C0-APX-093

Susan's
CHRISTMAS SHOP

Susan's
CHRISTMAS SHOP

Susan Topp Weber

Photographs by Blair Clark

Susan Topp Weber
Santa Fe

20 19 18 17 16 5 4 3 2 1

Designed by Virginia Snow
Printed and bound in Hong Kong

Library of Congress Cataloging-in-Publication Data

Names: Weber, Susan Topp, author.
Title: Susan's Christmas Shop / Susan Topp Weber.
Description: First Edition. | Layton, Utah : Gibbs Smith, 2016.
Identifiers: LCCN 2016000324 | ISBN 9781423639404 (hardcover)
Subjects: LCSH: Christmas decorations. | Handicraft. | Susan's Christmas
Shop.
Classification: LCC TT900.C4 W43 2016 | DDC 745.594/12--dc23
LC record available at http://lccn.loc.gov/2016000324
ISBN 13: 978-1-4236-3940-4

This book is dedicated to all the talented people who have made special handmade things for Susan's Christmas Shop over the years, and to all my customers, especially the man who told me, "I've been shopping here since before your hair turned grey!"

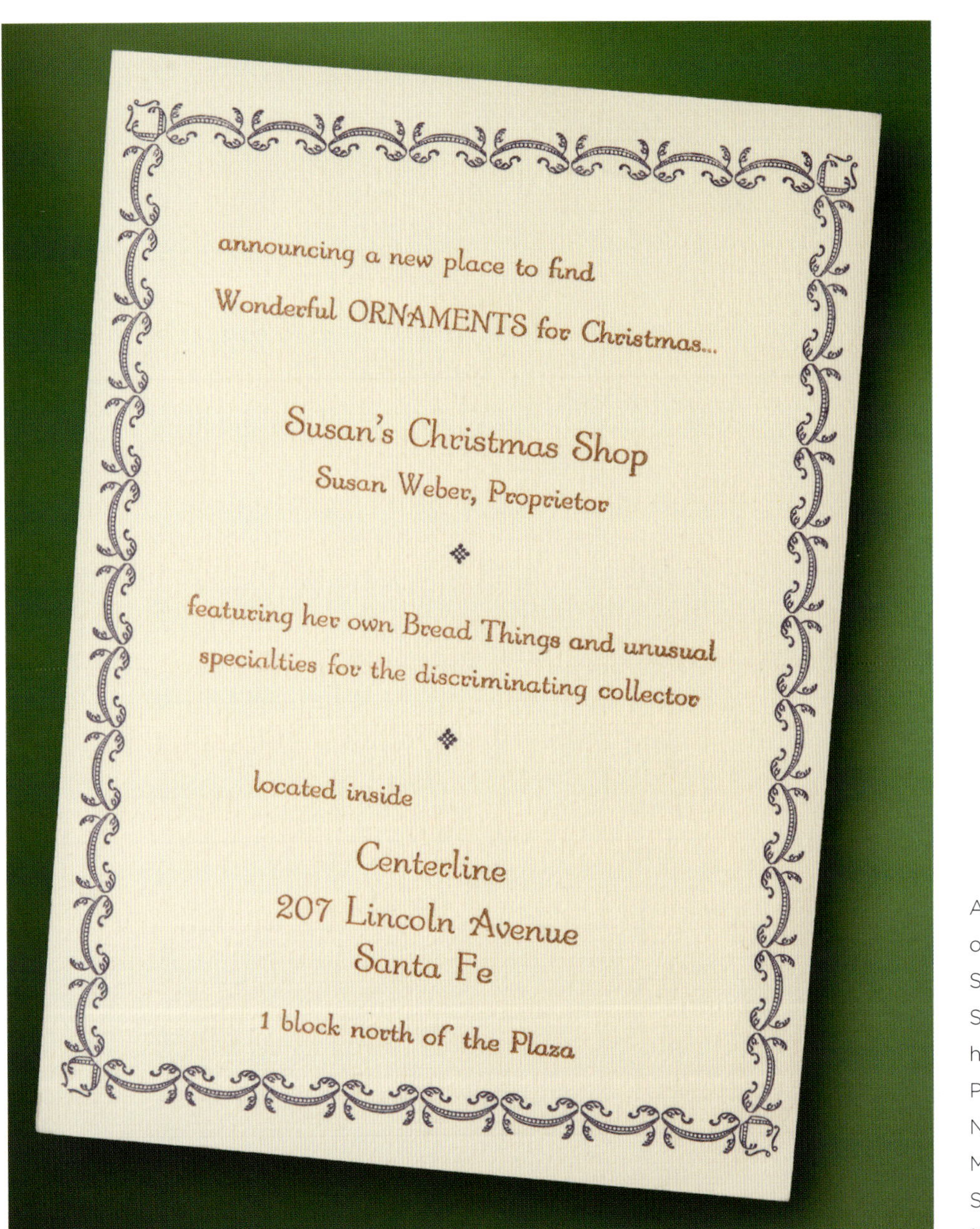

Announcement of the opening of Susan's Christmas Shop. Printed by hand at the Palace Press, part of the New Mexico History Museum, by Pam Smith, September 1978.

CONTENTS

FOREWORD

I love anything unique in Christmas decorations, and my whole life has been dedicated to trimming trees and designing themed exhibitions pertaining to Christmas fantasies, rituals, and celebrations; hence my sobriquet, Father Christmas.

On my first trip to Santa Fe in the 1970s, I discovered Susan's Christmas Shop. I was accustomed to visiting Christmas stores, but what a surprise to discover this tiny shop glowing with unusual treasures. I was totally captivated by its magic. Susan's store is like going back in time to an enchanted toy shop as seen in antique prints from the Victorian period.

Every inch of the shop was covered with unique, handmade objects, from ornaments to crèches to books and cards—all things I had never seen before! Over many years of shopping trips, I developed a friendship with Susan and became aware of her keen eye, her artistic talent, and her vast knowledge and expertise of what she sells—and most of all, her success as a shopkeeper extraordinaire.

Every trip to Santa Fe now includes a visit to Susan's Christmas Shop. Some of the distinctive miniature items I purchased at Susan's are now in vignettes in the Museum of Wonder & Delight in Folsom, California. This book will show many of the individual handmade gems Susan has offered over the years inside an old adobe room in historic downtown Santa Fe.

Father Christmas,
Dolph Gotelli
Creative Director/Curator
Museum of Wonder & Delight
Historic Folsom, California

18 in. (46 cm.) in diameter
Collection of Jody and Katherine Norskog,
Santa Fe, New Mexico

PREFACE

Susan's Christmas Shop has become a favorite Santa Fe landmark over many years—almost forty now. It is located in the heart of historic downtown Santa Fe. The shop blossomed when the right person, myself, met the right location, 115 East Palace Avenue.

Many things led to that meeting. I was born the second of ten children. My father was an officer in the United States Army, so we moved often. My father was stationed at Sandia Base in Albuquerque in the mid-1950s, and my parents grew to love New Mexico. When they could request an assignment again, my father had just finished a four-year tour of duty in Germany. All my high school years had been spent in Germany, a truly wonderful experience.

My father requested a reassignment to Sandia Base. My older sister and I had graduated from Frankfurt American High School and were ready for college, but I had eight younger siblings who would eventually need to go to college too, so I got a small scholarship, lived at home, and went to the local university, the University of New Mexico. Through a friend I met at UNM, I had a beautiful introduction to the Pueblo people of New Mexico. I formed lasting friendships at many of the pueblos. I now deal with Pueblo and Navajo Indians on a daily basis in my shop. I married and moved to Santa Fe in 1965. Two babies were born, a girl and a boy.

I realized at a young age that I prefer things that are made by hand. I have always loved Christmas, so my personal Christmas tree was full of special handmade ornaments and my collection of them was growing. My husband decided to pursue an advanced degree at UNM, and we moved back to Albuquerque. We lived in an apartment complex close to the university. This complex had a building where informal classes could be held. I heard that the YWCA was holding classes there, so I put my baby boy in a red wagon and held my toddler daughter's hand as we walked to the center. A craft class was being offered, but the tuition was out of my reach. Just as I started to pull my red wagon back to my apartment a woman from the YWCA said to me, "Wait. Would you be interested in this class?"

"Yes," I said, "but I have no money."

"If you have a few dollars to join the YWCA, I will pay your tuition," she said.

I was amazed. "Why would you do this for me?" I asked.

"When I was young, someone helped me," she said, "and I would like to pass that along."

We had never met before that morning, and she had no way of knowing how this class would change my life. As soon as my hands touched the simple salt dough, I knew this was my medium. The instructor became silent as she watched me create. Within a month I was selling my Christmas ornaments to a gift shop in Old Town, Albuquerque. The next summer I was accepted into the New Mexico Arts and Crafts Fair, an important juried craft show that has been a springboard for many local artists and craftsmen. Soon I had eager collectors who bought everything I made.

I never saw the woman from the YWCA again. But because of her, I have an obligation to help younger artists. Susan's Christmas Shop has given me a way to do this.

ACKNOWLEDGMENTS

I wish to thank the customers who responded to my request, searched through their personal collections, and loaned their favorites so they could be photographed for this book. These include Sandy Barnstorp, Rich Bozanich, Marilyn Brophy, Diana Bryer, Betty Chavez, Helen Gaus, Trudel Gifford, Linda Hamilton, Allane Holman, Sylvia Hughes, Liz King, Leah Kostoplos, Paula Krogdahl, Kenneth Leonard, Cindy Mares, Jody and Katherine Norskog, Donna Parker, Kathy Phelan, James McKay, Boo Miller, Ellen Sierocinski, Jason Trainor, and my daughter, Melissa Weber. I thank Blair Clark for his excellent photography. I also thank Michela Aveta and Kathy Phelan for their invaluable technical assistance, and Michela Aveta, Kent DeYoung, Kristy Gallegos, Leah Kostoplos, Susan McArthur, Joe Miracle, Hensley Peterson, Karen Sears, and Susan Summers for endlessly looking at photographs and making valuable suggestions. Thanks to Danny Gallegos for making the fresh evergreen garland hanging on the door on the front cover. Finally, I thank my son, Andrew Weber, for his special contribution to this book.

THE BEGINNING OF SUSAN'S CHRISTMAS SHOP

My husband and I moved back to Santa Fe in the early 1970s. By 1978, we had bought a two-story Victorian house on a hill overlooking downtown Santa Fe. This house appears on page 21 of my first book, *Christmas in Santa Fe.* The house had been a day-care center prior to our purchase, and was in need of restoration. Our purchase saved the house from being torn down, and we got it listed on national, state, and city registers of historic structures.

By this time, I had been making my own ornaments out of salt dough for nine years. I could do this at home after a day of work as a housewife, a mother of two small children, and a historic preservation worker. I called my creations "Bread Things." They were always Christmas ornaments made of the humble materials of flour, salt, and water. I formed them with my hands and simple tools like toothpicks, palette knives, and a garlic press. I typically worked at night when my two children were in bed, and I let the ornaments bake slowly all night. I sold my ornaments to a few Santa Fe gift shops and galleries, and sold them directly to the public at a few juried arts and crafts fairs in Albuquerque and Mesilla Park outside of Las Cruces.

In 1975, my work was accepted in a museum show called Craft Multiples at the Renwick Gallery, a branch of the Smithsonian in Washington, D.C. I had responded to a call for entries, which appeared in the local newspaper. My entry was a six-piece set of Christmas ornaments, which together comprised a nativity. I was the only New Mexican in this national show. Everything in the Craft Multiples show was purchased for the permanent collection of the Smithsonian, in order to document production craft in the United States at the time of the Bicentennial.

Because of my experience selling at arts and crafts fairs, I knew that I enjoyed dealing directly with the public. My husband suggested selling other handmade Christmas decorations in a shop of my own. We were still restoring the Victorian house and wanted to raise money for that project. The idea of a shop appealed to me. A family loan allowed me to go on my first buying trip to California.

The launch of Susan's Christmas Shop was originally planned for the summer of 1978, but it is the nature of life to be unpredictable. The day after I returned from that first buying trip, I was a passenger in the front seat of a car that was struck

DECORATED GOOSE EGG BY PAULA KROGDAHL (1988)

3 in. (7½ cm.) tall
Collection of Allane Holman,
Santa Fe, New Mexico

head-on by a fifteen-year-old drunk driver. The teenager died instantly. I spent weeks of recovery in an Albuquerque hospital, my jaw a broken jigsaw puzzle, my face full of stitches. My jaw was wired shut, but I was grateful to be alive and I knew I had a shop to open. For three months—October through December 1978—I rented a corner of a wonderful shop called Centerline on Lincoln Avenue, across the street from the Santa Fe City Hall. That address is now a parking lot, and only a few of my oldest customers remember my brief time there.

In keeping with my love of handmade things, the announcement of Susan's Christmas Shop was created by hand. It was printed at the Palace Press, which was located in a historic adobe building behind the Palace of the Governors. Pam Smith ran the Palace Press at that time. She set the antique type by hand, one letter at a time, and used a nineteenth-century printing press to print it. That press is still there, part of the New Mexico History Museum.

In this small corner of Centerline, I often painted my own Bread Things during store hours to keep busy and to create things to sell to my collectors.

It was at Centerline that Paula Krogdahl first offered for sale her beautiful eggshells decorated with distinctive Southwest designs. I instantly recognized Paula's talent. For many years, Paula's eggs were a staple in my shop. She would work on quail, chicken, turkey, and goose eggs, using a fine Rapidograph pen and black ink. Paula grew up in a large, historic adobe house in Corrales, New Mexico, close to the colonial San Ysidro Church and Casa San Ysidro, so she was familiar with Southwest design elements, but the way she put these designs onto the shell of an egg made them her own. She strung the eggs to hang, sometimes with feathers below.

BREAD THINGS BY SUSAN TOPP WEBER (1980s)

The angel (left center) is $2\frac{1}{2}$ in. ($6\frac{1}{2}$ cm.) tall

Collection of Kathy Phelan, Santa Fe, New Mexico

Paula eventually developed painful arthritis in her hands that ended her career of egg art. Thankfully, that arthritis is currently in remission. Paula now lives in Tesuque, just north of Santa Fe.

I recently learned that Paula had sat nervously in her car outside Centerline before gathering the courage to show me her eggs. I told her of my identical emotions the first time my own work was offered to a gift shop in 1969. I never made it out of the car. Instead, my good friend went in on my behalf. Paula's bravery led to a pattern of artists bringing their creations for me to see. I seem to have an ability to recognize talent, and to promote it. My motivating instinct might be expressed as "find beauty and share it." This book will document many locally made items, as well as handmade things from all over the world, which I have seen and selected to sell in my shop, from the very first years up to the present.

115 EAST PALACE AVENUE

At the end of December 1978, my shop in a corner of Centerline closed. A permanent location for Susan's Christmas Shop was needed. I thought of The Shed restaurant. I first ate lunch at The Shed in 1963. I loved the food and the creative atmosphere. I wanted my shop to be close to The Shed because I saw how people waited to get in there. On the eve of a trip to Europe, I learned that a small space *might* be available, but I was leaving very early the next morning. The negotiations were left in the hands of Ruth Weber, my mother-in-law, and when I returned two weeks later the space was mine. My new shop address would be 115 East Palace Avenue, where it has been ever since July 1979.

The little room I was able to rent, less than two hundred square feet, was perfect for me. It has thick adobe walls, a worn wooden floor, *vigas* (log beams) supporting wide boards above them, and a thick dirt roof above those boards. A dirt roof on an adobe building is a sign of great age. The room was part of an adobe house built around a central patio. This house first appeared on a map of Santa Fe in 1846, long before the much larger Sena Plaza was built to the east of my shop. L. Bradford Prince, chief justice of the New Mexico Territorial Supreme Court, purchased the house in 1879. The central patio of that house is now full of ancient trumpet vines, a vintage 'Austrian Copper' rose that blooms just once a year, but with great beauty, a flowering tree shaped like a leafy umbrella, several antique cast-iron benches, and Shed diners enjoying their meals beneath colorful umbrellas in the summer. This charming small patio bears L. Bradford's last name: Prince Patio.

To the west of my shop, closer to the plaza, is an even older adobe house, now called the Shop of the Rainbow Man. This house appears on the earliest known map of Santa Fe in 1766. Another adobe structure stood on that site before the Pueblo Revolt in 1680. East Palace Avenue is a very old part of Santa Fe.

In October 1880, President Rutherford B. Hayes and his wife, Lucy, visited Santa Fe. At that time, New Mexico was a territory of the United States. It was the first time a president of the United States had ever been to Santa Fe. Most of the local population gathered on the plaza to welcome him. There were patriotic tunes by the 9th Cavalry Band from Fort Wingate on the bandstand and there were speeches. The president's speech was not controversial, but then General William Tecumseh Sherman spoke. Among his other remarks, General Sherman said, "You must improve your land, and make the most of the resources that your location affords you, and you must get rid of your burros and goats. I hope ten years hence there won't be any adobe houses in the territory. I want you to learn to make them of brick, with slanting roofs. Yankees don't like flat roofs, nor roofs of dirt." All the other speeches that day drew applause. There was no applause for Sherman's speech, and the *Santa Fe New Mexican* wrote that General Sherman had "put his foot in it, as usual."

Photographer: Ben Wittick. 9th Cavalry Band on Plaza, Santa Fe, New Mexico, 1880. Courtesy of the Palace of the Governors Photo Archives (NMHM/DCA), 050887.

Later that day, President and Mrs. Hayes were guests at the home of L. Bradford Prince, now home to Susan's Christmas Shop and The Shed. Justice Prince showed off his personal library of New Mexico books and his collection of Indian relics. The president admired the cozy

and cheerful atmosphere, and the arrangement of adobe rooms opening onto the *placita,* the central patio. Lucy Hayes was charmed, and said that if she and her husband ever built a house again they would choose adobe.

In 1942, Martha Field purchased the two adjacent historic adobe houses on East Palace Avenue, which are now the Shop of the Rainbow Man and Prince Patio. World War II was in progress and patriotic feelings were high. Martha and her daughter turned Prince Patio into a service club for soldiers, and sold war bonds out of an office on the east side. In 1943, Martha leased the property at 109 East Palace Avenue to the University of California for a mysterious project related to the war. This is the famous address for all the physicists who worked secretly on the atomic bomb in Los Alamos. In the 1960s, I met Dorothy McKibbin, the woman who kept the office and met all the brilliant people, whose mission led them to the small door at the back of the long patio. Her office address was actually 109½ East Palace. Once they entered that door, they vanished. Dorothy took them out the back door and discretely got them to Los Alamos for their important work. After World War II ended, the two historic adobe properties became retail shops. The Shed restaurant moved from Burro Alley to its present location in 1960.

The small room at 115 East Palace, even though it is no longer a residence, continues to charm those who see it today. It is the ideal setting for the handmade treasures that have pleased my customers all these many years. There are two doors to Susan's Christmas Shop. One leads to the brick sidewalk on East Palace Avenue, covered with a portal painted a bright turquoise. The other door opens onto Prince Patio and the entrance to The Shed. Cabinets have been added inside the shop, and a Carpenter Gothic shelf with supporting posts provides storage "upstairs," so a ladder is essential. There is only one small window in the shop. It can be seen in the *zaguán*, the Spanish name for the passage, which is wide enough for a wagon to have been drawn into the courtyard in the colonial days. Now the *zaguán* is the inviting public entrance to Prince Patio, The Shed restaurant, and various other shops. The gate of the *zaguán* is closed late at night when the business of Prince Patio is done.

Not only is the property at Prince Patio historic, it is set into the heart of old Santa Fe, a few steps east of the historic plaza and the Palace of the Governors, the oldest public building in the United States. The long adobe palace was built in 1610 as the official government building of Santa Fe. Susan's Christmas Shop is within sight of the nineteenth-century stone Cathedral Basilica of St. Francis of Assisi and the tranquil Cathedral Park adjacent to it. It is close to the lovely Sena Plaza, with its mature trees, brick sidewalks, sheltered garden of flowers, elegant restaurant, and several small retail shops.

The present *portal*, or covered sidewalk, of the Palace of the Governors was not built until that building became a history museum in the early twentieth century. The Victorian-era *portal* of the Palace was torn down and replaced with what the builders presumed a Colonial portal might have looked like. Sena Plaza, east of Susan's Christmas Shop, did not have a *portal* at all until the mid-twentieth century. The other *portales* on the Santa Fe Plaza were built even later, so the *portal* outside Susan's Christmas Shop is probably the oldest in downtown Santa Fe.

THE EARLY YEARS AT 115 EAST PALACE AVENUE—THE GERMAN INFLUENCE

From the beginning, Susan's Christmas Shop has offered handmade Christmas decorations. Many of these came from Germany, which has a long tradition of decorating for Christmas. Since all my high school years were spent in Germany, I was familiar with German Christmas traditions, and fond of them. I sought handmade German Christmas decorations at the California Gift Show in Los Angeles in July 1978 from importers like Rolf Wallach, a fine German gentleman, now deceased.

After World War II, Germany was divided into the German Democratic Republic (East Germany) and the Federal Republic of Germany (West Germany). East Germany included a region called the Erzgebirge, south of Dresden along the Czech border. The name *Erzgebirge* translates as Ore Mountains. This region was known for its rich silver ore deposits, and mining was once an important industry there. When the fortunes of mining declined, many former miners began to use the resources that were aboveground—the trees that cover the Ore Mountains. They began to make wooden ornaments and figures, using lathe-turned pieces of wood glued together, as well as decorative incense burners called "Smoking Men."

The Erzgebirge was very isolated and remained a poor region after World War II. The East German government took over most of the businesses, and the style of the handwork they produced changed very little until Germany became one country again. For a few decades I could purchase traditional Erzgebirge work at low prices—prices kept artificially low by the heavy hand of the East German government. After Germany's reunification, the prices increased dramatically, but the fine traditional handwork of the region continues to this day.

WOODEN CHRISTMAS ORNAMENTS FROM GERMANY (1980s)

The chimney sweep is 3 in. ($7^1/_2$ cm.) tall
Collections of Sylvia Hughes, Albuquerque, New Mexico (center), and James McKay, Santa Fe, New Mexico (left and right)

The ornaments here are a combination of East and West German handwork. The chimney sweep pull-toy ornament is from the Erzgebirge. In Germany, it is considered good luck to see an old-fashioned chimney sweep. His arms and legs move when the string is pulled. The Christmas tree and snowman on a sled ornaments are made by a family business called Christian Ulbricht. The Ulbricht family managed to escape from East Germany to Bavaria and prospered there. Eventually the family was able to buy back the original company in Seiffen, the famous picturesque little town in the heart of the Erzgebirge.

WOODEN SMOKING MAN FROM EAST GERMANY (1980)

The chimney is 3 in. (7½ cm.) tall
Collection of Sylvia Hughes,
Albuquerque, New Mexico

This smoking man is actually a wooden chimney with a small wooden chimney sweep and his ladder. The chimney lifts up. A cone of incense is set on a metal plate beneath the chimney and lit. When the chimney is replaced over the lit incense, the smoke of the incense comes out the chimney. Holes in the wood allow air to circulate and keep the incense actively burning for several minutes. On the bottom of the wooden base of this smoking man is stamped "German Democratic Republic," the official name of the former East Germany. It was sold at Susan's Christmas Shop in 1980.

DOE AND FAWN RING ANIMALS FROM THE ERZGEBIRGE, GERMANY (1982)

The doe is 2 in. (5 cm.) tall
Collection of Melissa Weber, Tucson, Arizona

The Erzgebirge woodworkers use a technique that is unique to that region. A smooth tree trunk is put on a lathe. Using a lathe, a ring of wood is created with a specific profile. Skillful lathe operators can make very detailed rings. Then the rings are sliced into many segments. Each slice has a profile carefully created by the lathe worker. The sliced pieces are then carved by hand to look like the three-dimensional animal the lathe worker visualized while working on the ring. Finally the carved slices of wood are tinted. This wonderful doe and fawn are both ring animals, made from two different rings. The doe's ears are separate pieces of wood added to the ring animal. This challenging specialized woodworking technique still exists in the Erzgebirge.

NOAH'S ARK WITH RING ANIMALS FROM THE ERZGEBIRGE, GERMANY (2015)

The ark is 5 in. (12½ cm.) tall
Susan's Christmas Shop, Santa Fe, New Mexico

Noah's ark was a popular toy in the nineteenth century, since it was based on a biblical story and therefore suitable for children's Sunday playtime. All the various animals in this scene are ring animals, fashioned in the Erzgebirge from slices of many rings of wood turned on a lathe. Noah and his family are tiny figures made of lathe-turned pieces of wood, carefully cut, glued together, and then tinted. A good-quality Noah's ark like this one always brings a good price because of the large number of figures and the amount of time and care given to creating them, either one by one or, perhaps in this case, two by two.

NUREMBERG ANGEL FROM GERMANY (1982)

12 in. (30½ cm.) tall

Collection of Sylvia Hughes, Albuquerque, New Mexico

In Nuremberg, Germany, it is customary for a young girl dressed in an angel costume to open the famous Nuremberg Christmas Market. Many small replicas of Nuremberg angels are made there, some as Christmas ornaments and some as tree tops. The heads of these angels are often made of molded wax or porcelain. Their hair might be real and their dresses are often made of pleated gold foil.

This German tree-top angel is the best of the Nuremberg angels. Her face and hands are made of wax, her wings are real feathers, and her hair is real hair. Her dress is made of the finest fabrics. She can be the crowning glory of a Christmas tree, or look elegant sitting on a mantle. This angel was purchased in my shop in the early 1980s.

WOODEN ANGEL MUSICIANS BY WENDT & KÜHN (2015)

The conductor and podium is 3 in. (7½ cm.) tall
Susan's Christmas Shop, Santa Fe, New Mexico

Wendt & Kühn is a famous German company that has been making charming painted wooden figures for a hundred years. It all began in 1913, when Grete Wendt entered a design competition. Her creation of a trio of berry-picking children won second prize. Two years later, Grete and her friend Grete Kühn formed a partnership and workshop. Both young women were graduates of the Royal Saxon School of Applied Art in Dresden. Grete Wendt's award-winning berry-picking children had been featured in several magazines, which resulted in many orders for the new business.

Wendt & Kühn is located in a historic half-timbered building in Grünhainichen, a small village at the edge of the Erzgebirge, south of Dresden. After World War II, Grünhainichen was part of East Germany. Wendt & Kühn was taken over by the East German government, but it managed to retain the W&K initials during those years. Eventually East and West Germany were reunited, and in 1990 the company was back in the hands of the family that started it. Today the work by Wendt & Kühn is considered the finest of German wooden figures.

The angel musicians made by Wendt & Kühn have trademark green wings with eleven white dots. The first angel was made by the company in 1923. The angels wear nothing but a little white shirt. Because they are designed with separate pieces of wood to make their limbs, they are less stiff looking than traditional Erzgebirge folk art. Many of these angels play musical instruments, led by a conductor on a podium.

PEWTER ORNAMENTS FROM GERMANY (1982)

The *Christkind* (left) is 3 in. (7½ cm.) tall
Collection of the author, Santa Fe, New Mexico

Pewter ornaments have been made in Germany for a very long time. The molds for pewter ornaments are carved by hand into pieces of slate. Then the molten pewter is poured into the mold. When the pewter is cool, the ornament is removed from the mold, cleaned up, and painted. The molds used to make these ornaments are quite old. The one on the left is a Christ child, or *Christkind.* The one on the right is a Nuremberg angel, the special angel that opens the Christmas Market in that famous German city. The central ornament has angels playing heavenly music. The painting on the pewter is quite detailed.

PEWTER WINTER FOREST SCENE BY WILHELM SCHWEIZER (2015)

The tallest tree is 8 in. (20¼ cm.)
Susan's Christmas Shop, Santa Fe, New Mexico

Wilhelm Schweizer is an innovative pewter company in Dießen am Ammersee. Ammersee is a large lake southwest of Munich. The painted pewter standing pieces shown here are all of a contemporary design. The molds for these pieces are also carved by hand into slate and cast in the same way as the vintage-style ornaments, but at Wilhelm Schweizer, every year several new styles are introduced. Wilhelm Schweizer-painted pewter figures are one of the most popular German products offered at Susan's Christmas Shop, because they can be used to make elaborate scenes for Christmas and Easter. The pewter trees can create a forest in a green summer style or a cold, snowy winter style, suitable for Santa to stride through on his way to work.

WAX CHRISTMAS ORNAMENTS (1985)

The wax Santa is 4 in. (10 cm.) tall
Collection of Sylvia Hughes, Albuquerque, New Mexico

Christmas ornaments made of wax are usually from Austria or Germany. Wax ornaments are mentioned as early as 1800. They are molded in a one-piece mold so that they are always flat on the back. When the wax cools and hardens, they are carefully painted by hand. The hearts in the photo are from Austria. The wax Santa ornament was made in the United States. In the 1980s, a woman in Chicago was using a nice collection of vintage Austrian wax molds to create her own special line of wax ornaments. Her carefully painted wax ornaments are no longer being made, and the whereabouts of her molds is unknown. I have not seen wax ornaments offered at trade shows for many years.

FLOCKED DEER FIGURES BY WAGNER HANDWORK COMPANY (1990)

3 in. (7½ cm.) long
Collection of Sylvia Hughes, Albuquerque, New Mexico

The Wagner Handwork Company in Germany made delightful flocked animals for many years. They were ideal for children to play with because they were so durable. On labels placed beneath the animals, the company proudly declared that the work was "HANDWORK," made by hand in West Germany. Unfortunately, the German company is no longer in business, unable to compete with cheaper Chinese-made animals. Susan's Christmas Shop sold the flocked German animals in the 1980s and 1990s. When I learned that Wagner would stop making them, I made sure both of my grandsons, Ricky and Mike, had enough reindeer to pull a sleigh driven by a small Santa.

CARVED WOODEN CHILD'S NATIVITY FROM GERMANY (2012)

The tallest king is almost 5 in. (12½ cm.)
Susan's Christmas Shop, Santa Fe, New Mexico

This hand-carved nativity set has been made by four generations of one German family since 1929. There are many different pieces representing humans, angels, and animals. Each piece is hand carved and then stained. They are appropriate for children to handle without concern that they will break. The figures are sold individually, so it easily becomes a cherished family tradition to add a piece or two each year for Christmas. Susan's Christmas Shop has sold this nativity since the 1980s. I'm giving both my grandsons a piece or two each Christmas, so when they are grown up they will each have a large and distinctive nativity set.

EARLY LOCAL ARTISTS AND ARTISANS

At Susan's Christmas Shop, German specialties and other international items have always been combined with the creations of various local artists. Sometimes I found the artists and sometimes they found me, but when their work pleased me I added it to the inventory. Meanwhile, I continued to make my own Bread Things for the shop.

PUEBLO POT REPLICA ORNAMENTS BY SUSAN TOPP WEBER (1979)

Typical pot is 1½ in. (4 cm.) tall (the size of a large walnut)
Collection of the author, Santa Fe, New Mexico

In 1979, my mother, Mary Catherine Topp, became New Mexico's Mother of the Year. My parents lived in Santa Fe at that time. Mother had to travel to New York City, taking with her a gift for every other State Mother of the Year. It was her idea that I make the gifts, and it was also her idea that they should be replicas of New Mexican pueblo pots. I had been making my bread-dough ornaments for about ten years. At first I did not want to make the Pueblo pots because they were not my own original designs. But when your mother asks you, and when she is New Mexico's Mother of the Year, you cannot say no. Once I made fifty-five pots for her, I was hooked. I collect Pueblo pottery, and I love the traditional and innovative designs painted by anonymous Pueblo women years ago. My tiny pot ornaments require concentration and hours of time, but they are quite satisfying to make and amazing to see.

HAND-PAINTED STONEWARE ORNAMENTS BY MARY JULYAN (1980)

Ornaments are 3 in. ($7^1/_2$ cm.) tall
Collection of Helen Gaus, Tucson, Arizona

Mary Julyan lived in Albuquerque, New Mexico. She made these hand-painted ornaments out of stoneware. The ornament with a blue bird is St. Francis of Assisi, the popular patron saint of Santa Fe. He represents the Catholicism brought to New Mexico by the Spanish colonists centuries ago. The other ornament is a Blue Corn Maiden, inspired by the Pueblo reverence for corn. Mary made these two popular ornaments for my shop for many years, from 1980 to 1990, but once her children were out of school she retired. Mary and her husband then took trips to England to hike in the countryside.

PIÑON WOODEN ORNAMENTS WITH WOODBURNED DESIGNS BY SUSIE MOUCHETTE (EARLY 1980s)

2½ in. (6¼ cm.) in diameter
Collections of Melissa Weber, Tucson, Arizona (two ornaments on left), and the author, Santa Fe, New Mexico (two ornaments on right)

Susie Mouchette was a young woman living in Santa Fe when she made these ornaments for my shop in small quantities in the early 1980s. Her father sliced piñon branches in a way that kept the bark on the slice. Then Susie used a hot woodburning tool to burn the Southwest designs on both sides of the ornament, a very slow process. Once Susie's father died, Susie found it difficult to get good slices of wood, and so there were no more of these charming ornaments. Susie's ornaments are treasures.

TEASEL ORNAMENTS (1980s)

2½ in. (6¼ cm.) tall
Collection of Rich Bozanich, Rancho Palos Verdes, California

Teasels are dried seedpods of a plant not found in New Mexico; they come from the Midwest. For a few years, teasels were used to make limited quantities of amusing novelty Christmas ornaments. Here is a tourist teasel with his map, tourist information, and camera, just like thousands of tourists who come to Santa Fe. The other teasel ornament is a Sugarplum Fairy. These were sold at Susan's Christmas Shop in the 1980s. Teasel ornaments are no longer being offered at wholesale gift shows.

COTTON BOLE ANGEL BY PATTI LATIMER (mid-1980s)

The cotton bole angel is 3 in. (7½ cm.) tall
Collection of Boo Miller, Santa Fe, New Mexico

Della Beth Leonard lived in Lubbock, Texas, but regularly came to Santa Fe. She would eat at The Shed and visit my shop, occasionally offering ornaments made by her daughter and son-in-law. Della's daughter, Patti Latimer, made angel ornaments using cotton boles. These ornaments were popular and we sold many cotton bole angels for several years.

PAINTED STARFISH SANTA AND MERMAID ORNAMENTS BY LOUIS COSTABEL (mid-1980s)

The starfish Santa is 4 in. (10 cm.) tall
Collections of Kenneth Leonard, Lubbock, Texas (left), and the author, Santa Fe, New Mexico (right)

Della Leonard also had a son-in-law, Louis Costabel, who lived on Martha's Vineyard with another of Della's daughters. For one or two seasons in the mid-1980s, hundreds of starfish washed up on Martha's Vineyard beaches. Louis collected many of these starfish, dried them, painted them to look like Santas, and made them into hanging Christmas ornaments. He sent some of them to Della, and she offered them to my shop. These ornaments always had a delightful, animated look, and there were never two alike. Eventually the starfish moved to other coastal waters, and I could no longer get these amusing starfish Santa ornaments for my shop.

About the same time as Susan's Christmas Shop sold starfish Santa ornaments, a local artist made ornaments of sweet little mermaids holding a tiny starfish or a seashell. This was so long ago now that the name of the artist is lost. This particular mermaid's tail needed to be repaired before she could be photographed, but she continues to delight.

KACHINA ORNAMENTS BY ELSIE MORALES (1980s)

Typical ornament is 2½ in. (6¼ cm.) tall
Collection of Liz King, Santa Fe, New Mexico

Elsie Morales began making detailed *kachina* ornaments of colored polymer clay and feathers when she was a housewife living in White Rock in the 1980s. Her ornaments became very popular and very collectible. Elsie always added feathers and accessories to her *kachina* figures, which added to their appeal. Each ornament had a name, such as Sun Kachina and the clown Koshari with his watermelon. Elsie is not a Pueblo Indian herself, but she was inspired by *kachinas* she saw in books. Eventually Elsie's life changed and she moved away from New Mexico. She no longer makes *kachina* ornaments, but customers continued to ask for her work for many years, and collectors can tell you proudly how many Elsie Morales *kachina* ornaments they own.

SOUTHWEST TREE-TOP ANGEL BY DELIA SCHERTLER (1988)

10 in. (25½ cm.) tall
Collection of Sylvia Hughes,
Albuquerque, New Mexico

Delia Schertler was born in Ayacucho, Peru, where she met and married an American man and moved to Albuquerque, New Mexico. When she was a housewife, Delia designed this Southwest tree-top angel. The angel has a cone base without legs, so it can sit on a table or the top of a tree. Delia also made smaller stuffed Southwest angels as Christmas ornaments in a similar style and fabric. Later she started a career in real estate and no longer makes ornaments and tree tops, but they enriched my shop for a few years in the 1980s.

SANTA AND MRS. CLAUS TIN ORNAMENTS BY KAT DANCER (1990s)

4 1/4 in. (11 cm.) tall
Collection of the author, Santa Fe, New Mexico

Kat Dancer was a Santa Fe craftswoman who cut Santa figures out of tin, which she then painted. They were made as Christmas ornaments, but also as standing figures in two sizes. Mrs. Santa could chase Santa with a list of the good boys and girls, and Kat often supplied blank paper lists, so that the first names of family members could be written on them. Eventually Kat moved to another state and stopped making her Santa figures, but many of them were sold at Susan's Christmas Shop in the early 1990s.

MARBLEIZED PAPER DRAGON ORNAMENT BY PAM SMITH (1982) / CUT-PAPER ORNAMENTS BY MICHELLE TSOSIE SISNEROS (2002)

The dragon is almost 4 in. (10 cm.) tall; the female paper figure is 6 in. (15¼ cm.) tall
Collection of the author, Santa Fe, New Mexico

Pam Smith worked at the Palace Press behind the Palace of the Governors in the 1980s. Historically, distinctive endpapers for finer books were made using marbleized paper. Pam used to demonstrate the technique of marbleizing paper at the Palace Press, with large trays of thick fluid and various colored inks and pigments floating on the surface. These pigments could be manipulated with various stirring tools and combs to create unique patterns. When she was satisfied with the appearance of the pigments, Pam carefully lowered a large sheet of special damp paper onto the surface of the fluid, captured the pigments on the surface of the paper, lifted up the transformed paper, and set it aside to dry. From sheets of this marbleized paper glued onto both sides of cardboard, Pam made the dragon ornament (center). Some of Pam's ornaments and pins were sold at Susan's Christmas Shop in the 1980s. Pam retired from the Palace Press many years ago. She created the design reproduced on this book's endsheets.

Michelle Tsosie Sisneros is a talented artist from Santa Clara Pueblo, near Española, New Mexico. In the 1980s and 1990s, Michelle made cut-paper ornaments and bookmarks in a distinctive contemporary Southwest style. She added paint to the surface of each one, so all of them were artistic, lightweight, and unique. Michelle has turned her artistic talent to painting in recent years, but at my request she now plans to make her paper ornaments again.

Dear John
I heard you ask daddy what I was like & where I lived. I have drawn ME & My House for you. Take care of the picture. I am just off now for Oxford with my bundle of toys — some for you. Hope I shall arrive in time: the snow is very thick at the NORTH POLE tonight: Yr loving Fr. Chr.
Love to daddy, mummy, michael & auntie & mary
Christmas House, North Pole
22nd December 1920
Dear John
I heard you ask daddy what I was like and where I lived. I have drawn me and my house for you. Take care of the picture. I am just off now for Oxford with my bundle of toys – some for you. Hope I shall arrive in time: the snow is very thick at the North Pole tonight. Your loving Father Christmas
FROM FATHER CHRISTMAS
ME
FC
MY HOUSE
FC

PAGES FROM *LETTERS FROM FATHER CHRISTMAS* BY J. R. R. TOLKIEN, PUBLISHED BY HOUGHTON MIFFLIN (2004)

The book is 111 pages, hardcover, 7¼ x 9½ in. (18½ x 24 cm.)
Collection of the author, Santa Fe, New Mexico

J. R. R. Tolkien was born in England close to the end of the nineteenth century. He had a long career as an academic at Oxford, but he also wrote stories for children. He is famous for his books *The Hobbit* and *The Lord of the Rings,* which have been translated into more than forty languages and have been read by millions of readers. When Tolkien married and had children of his own, he began writing delightful letters to them, anonymously from Father Christmas. Once a year in December the letters would arrive at the Tolkien house, bearing a stamp from the North Pole. They would be written in a wobbly hand, like the handwriting of an old man. They would tell stories of adventures at the North Pole, with illustrations. They were all signed Father Christmas. The first letter was written in 1920, when John, Tolkien's oldest child, was three years old. Eventually there were four children in the Tolkien family. The last letter was written in 1943. It must have been fun to grow up in that family. Susan's Christmas Shop has sold several different versions of *Letters from Father Christmas* over the years. The one shown here is one of the best.

HANDMADE *NISSE* FIGURES (1980s)

3 in. (7½ cm.) tall
Collection of the author, Santa Fe, New Mexico

There are tiny, beloved, magical elfin creatures in Scandinavia called *nisses*. They can appear any time of year, but they are especially associated with Christmas. A talented Los Alamos housewife with a Scandinavian lineage created her handmade versions of *nisses* for a year or two, and sold them to Susan's Christmas Shop in the late 1980s. The little elves usually wear tall, pointed, red felt hats. These also have glass bead eyes and sometimes carry embroidered felt hearts. There is wire inside their arms and legs, so they can be placed in lifelike positions. They are placed on a tiny round piece of wood as a base. These *nisse* figures have not been made for many years.

VICTORIAN-STYLE BUCKET AND CONE ORNAMENTS (1992)

The bucket is 6 1/2 in. (16 1/2 cm.) tall
Collection of the author, Santa Fe, New Mexico

During the nineteenth century, paper scraps, elegant gold foil decorative elements, fancy ribbons, and bows were combined to make containers that could be hung on the Christmas tree to hold sweets or small gifts. One man in New York City made exact reproductions of these Victorian-style ornaments on his kitchen table. I found them in New York and sold them at Susan's Christmas Shop in the late 1980s.

COLORED DOUGH ORNAMENTS BY VANNI LOWDENSLAGER (1984)

Winged Soul is 3½ in. (9 cm.) tall
Collections of Sylvia Hughes, Albuquerque, New Mexico (left), and the author, Santa Fe, New Mexico (center and right)

Vanni Lowdenslager is from Gunnison, Colorado. In the 1970s, Vanni saw Ecuadorian ornaments made of colored dough and tried to create original designs in dough herself. Vanni invented her own recipe for the dough. She makes it with bits of soft white bread and white Elmer's glue. The resulting mixture is kneaded until it becomes smooth. After Vanni forms each dough ornament it must dry. During the lengthy drying process the ornament shrinks a great deal, about 40 percent. Sometimes Vanni puts pigment in the dough before she forms it, and sometimes she paints the dough after it is completely dry. Vanni has now worked for decades in this medium, and her style has evolved over that time. The ornaments pictured here are typical of Vanni's early work. The center ornament here is called Winged Soul.

TATTED RING ORNAMENTS (1980s)

The large ring is 5 in. (12 1/2 cm.) in diameter
Collection of the author, Santa Fe, New Mexico

Tatting is a type of knotting. The technique of tatting curiosities was popular with sailors in their leisure time, because they were already quite familiar with different types of knots in their daily work with sails. Victorian ladies used the same tatting technique, but they used a finer thread, and worked primarily to make a dainty, lacy edge to a handkerchief or dresser scarf. These bold tatted ornaments were made in the 1980s. The name of the man who made them is now lost.

SANTA CLAUS STICK ORNAMENTS BY RUTH CARRAWAY (1990s)

The Santa face ornament is 5 in. (12½ cm.) tall
Collection of the author, Santa Fe, New Mexico

Ruth Carraway lives in the Sandia Mountains east of Albuquerque. She had a career in special education, but she has always created art in her spare time. She walked her mountain land, picked up sticks, and sculpted Santa faces onto them with polymer clay. The faces seem to have a live presence in them. Ruth attached wires so they can hang as ornaments. These were made in the 1990s. They are no longer made today.

CLAY POTTERY ORNAMENTS BY MICHELLE AND DARYL CANDELARIA (1980s)

The angel is 2½ in. (6½ cm.) tall
Collections of the author, Santa Fe, New Mexico (left), and Sylvia Hughes, Albuquerque, New Mexico (right)

Michelle and Daryl Candelaria are a sister and brother in a talented family from San Felipe Pueblo in New Mexico. San Felipe Pueblo is located on the Rio Grande almost halfway between Albuquerque and Santa Fe. The pottery ornaments are both made of native clay dug from the earth. Michelle no longer makes ornaments, such as her angel shown here, but Daryl has made some larger prize-winning pots since his little Pueblo drummer boy was made in the 1980s.

PAINTED WOODEN ORNAMENTS BY ROBERT TOLONE (1990) / PAINTED WOODEN BLOCK ORNAMENT BY MICHELLE McNEIL (1991)

The block is 2 in. (5 cm.) square and the elk is 3 in. (7½ cm.) tall
Collections of the author, Santa Fe, New Mexico (left), and
Wendy Grudzien, Healdsburg, California (center and right)

The ornaments that Robert Tolone produced through his Hang 'em High Designs have delighted many customers of Susan's Christmas Shop. In the mid-1980s, Robert had just finished art school at the Pratt Institute in New York and the Art Center College of Design in Pasadena, California, and he was looking for ways to make money. He had made a few painted wooden animal ornaments as gifts for friends. They encouraged him to make more and sell them. Soon his ornaments were being sold in fine shops and museums, and they had a clever name: Hang 'em High Designs.

Robert discovered that he could not meet the growing demand for his colorful animal ornaments by himself. Somehow he found Mr. Kim Boo Ho, a master carver in Seoul, South Korea. Mr. Kim had the skill to make high-quality, hand-carved, hand-painted wooden ornaments based on Robert's original designs. For a few years thousands of ornaments were made, and Susan's Christmas Shop was the top retailer of them.

Eventually Mr. Kim retired, and no one with his talent could be found to continue the work. The quality of the ornaments declined. Hang 'em High Designs closed, but Robert Tolone's distinctive wooden ornaments are still treasured by collectors. In 1989, there were thirty-six different original Robert Tolone animal designs. Robert still lives in Southern California and continues to sculpt as an artist.

The block-shaped ornament (left) is an original design by Michelle McNeil, who was married to Robert Tolone for many years.

TREE-TOP ANGEL BY DONNA GOEBEL (1991)

20 in. (51 cm.) tall
Collection of the author, Santa Fe, New Mexico

Donna Goebel lived in Taos, New Mexico. She made distinctive tree-top angels in the late 1980s and early 1990s, using antique quilts and vintage fabrics. Her angels had stiff fabric wings accented with gold, beautifully painted faces, decorative rickrack, ribbons, and lace edges. Sometimes the angels would hold a crystal, bird, bouquet, or some other decorative item. These angels could either be placed on top of a Christmas tree or be displayed on a solid wooden block. The blocks had a tall wooden dowel pegged into them, to invisibly support the angel inside the fabric. Donna made her angels in two sizes. This one is large, and the silk fabric is oriental. Health problems caused Donna to stop making these lovely angels in the 1990s.

MICE DOUGH ORNAMENTS BY VANNI LOWDENSLAGER (LATE 1980s)

1½ in. (4 cm.) tall
Collections of Karen Sears, Santa Fe, New Mexico (left), and
Melissa Weber, Tucson, Arizona (center and right)

These delightful mice were made by Vanni Lowdenslager in the late 1980s, using her special dough of bits of soft white bread and Elmer's glue. By this time Vanni's style had evolved to include several small three-dimensional figures such as pigs, penguins, kangaroos, and mice. These figures could stand or hang as ornaments. However, the three-dimensional style introduced frustrating new challenges. The thicker the dough, the longer the drying time, and the greater the risk of the figures developing cracks. As the years passed, Vanni continued to evolve her style. She began to make thinner, more two-dimensional ornaments. Now Vanni's fully rounded mouse wives and mouse mothers with whiskers are treasured even more because they are no longer made. They are irreplaceable.

SLIP-CAST ACOMA ORNAMENTS BY PRISCILLA JIM (2015)

The large bell is 2 in. (5 cm.) tall
Susan's Christmas Shop, Santa Fe, New Mexico

Priscilla Jim lives in Acomita, one of the villages below the ancient pueblo of Acoma, an hour's drive west of Albuquerque. She paints traditional Acoma pottery designs onto white slip-cast bells and cats. She uses the traditional black paint for Acoma pots, made from a native plant called Rocky Mountain beeweed. This plant is boiled down to make the black paint. Sometimes the paint is poured into a small corn husk basin to cool. If it cools in the pot it is tough to remove. The corn husk acts as a disposable palette for the paint.

Priscilla's bells and cats have been among the most popular ornaments at Susan's Christmas Shop since the 1980s. Priscilla delivers her work to my house before 8:00 a.m., after a two-hour drive from Acomita. Then we talk like old friends. I recently learned that her late grandmother, Frances Torivio, made a large Acoma pot in my collection. Frances Torivio is considered a matriarch of Acoma pottery. Perhaps Priscilla inherited her grandmother's painting skills.

SARATOGA SWEETS
The Peppermint Pig®
Net Wt. 8 Oz (224g)

PEPPERMINT PIG CANDY BY MIKE FITZGERALD (2015)

4 in. (10 cm.) long
Collection of the author, Santa Fe, New Mexico

In Saratoga Springs, New York, in the 1880s, a candymaker was looking for a novel new shape to mold his peppermint candy. He thought of a pig shape, perhaps because he was German, and pigs are a symbol of good luck in Germany. He molded white peppermint candy into several sizes of pigs, and hired schoolgirls to paint red stripes onto the white peppermint pigs on Saturdays. They used a red dye derived from beets. The pigs became very popular at Christmastime, and children looked forward to the special ceremony at the end of Christmas dinner, when the head of the family would place the peppermint pig in a small red pouch and smash it with a hammer. Everyone around the table would share a piece of the sweet, old-fashioned candy for good health, happiness, and prosperity in the coming new year. Eventually the candymaker retired and the peppermint pigs were no longer made, but they lived on in the memories of the oldest residents of Saratoga Springs.

In the 1990s, the local historical society asked Mike Fitzgerald, a modern candymaker, to revive the peppermint pig tradition. He agreed to do this, and he worked till late at night making peppermint candy pigs in three sizes. It was on a rainy morning that the peppermint pigs were to be offered in his candy shop for the first time. As he drank his breakfast coffee, Mike noticed a small story about the peppermint pigs on the front page of his newspaper. As he neared his shop that morning, he saw a crowd of people beneath umbrellas, gathered in front of his shop in the rain. At first he thought that perhaps there had been an accident, then realized that the people were all waiting to get into his candy shop. Mike noticed that they were mostly older people, who had enjoyed peppermint pigs in their childhood and wanted to enjoy them again. He got many letters of thanks from them. The pigs are no longer white peppermint striped by hand; they are now all bubblegum pink, but they are just as sweet as ever. The peppermint pig shown here was made by Mike Fitzgerald especially for this book.

CARVED BARK ORNAMENT (1980s)

2½ in. (6¼ cm.) wide
Collection of Helen Gaus, Tucson, Arizona

In Mexico, the bark of a certain tree is carved to make little fantasy houses as ornaments and sculptures. A young Mexican carver offered some of these carvings to me in the late 1980s. I suggested that she carve the bark in a Pueblo style of architecture instead of the Mexican fantasy style. This suggestion led to a new career for her, and later for her American husband as well. Her husband even invented new Southwest designs to sell. Susan's Christmas Shop sold these carvings for several years from the 1990s to the first years of the twenty-first century. The ornament shown here represents a trading post.

SILLY CHILE ORNAMENTS BY DIANA BRYER (1980s–1990s)

The Pirate Silly Chile (right) is 5½ in. (14 cm.) tall
Collection of Sandy Barnstorp, Yorba Linda, California

Diana Bryer is a self-taught artist who was born in Los Angeles, California, but moved to New Mexico in the 1980s. She now lives in Santa Cruz, New Mexico, close to Española. For several years, Diana made ornaments she sculpted out of polymer clay. Some of them were shaped like the red chiles so beloved to New Mexicans, but Diana gave them individual personalities and called them Silly Chiles. The ornaments in this photograph are a Bird Watcher Silly Chile, a Low Rider Silly Chile, and a Pirate Silly Chile (left to right). The Bird Watcher is one of a kind, made at the request of a customer. There were countless other styles as well. Diana's creative sense of humor always shows in her Silly Chiles. These were made in the 1980s and 1990s.

PAINTED BUFFALO GOURDS BY CATHLEEN KARDAS (1993, 2006)

The largest gourd is 2¾ in. (7 cm.) in diameter
Collections of Leah Kostoplos, Santa Fe, New Mexico (center), and the author, Santa Fe, New Mexico (left and right)

Cathleen Kardas moved to Albuquerque in 1973. She saw buffalo gourds growing wild on the mesa and had the idea to paint them with Southwest designs in 1977. She collects the buffalo gourds in the spring, after they have dried outdoors all winter. Her husband prepares the surface of the gourds using an elaborate procedure Cathleen invented, so that Cathleen's Rapidograph pen and acrylic paint can adhere to the gourd. Cathleen's designs reflect Pueblo pottery designs, prehistoric Mimbres pottery designs, or her original designs of horses, quails, and hummingbirds. Her gourds have been one of the most popular items at Susan's Christmas Shop since she began selling there in the 1980s. Cathleen made these gourds in 1993 and 2006. She now sells them exclusively to Susan's Christmas Shop.

SPANISH COLONIAL-STYLE *NICHO* AND NATIVITY, REPRODUCED FROM THE ORIGINAL BY CHARLIE CARRILLO (1988)

14 in. (35½ cm.) tall

Collection of Sylvia Hughes, Albuquerque, New Mexico

Charlie Carrillo is a well-known Santa Fe *santero. Santero* is an invented word used colloquially in New Mexico for a maker of religious art in the regional style called Spanish Colonial. Charlie has sold his original work in the summer Spanish Market for many years and has taught many of the artists who participate in that market. It is held on the plaza of Santa Fe in late July. A winter Spanish Market is held in November in Albuquerque.

As the prices of Charlie's original works of art increased, a market for an affordable reproduction developed. Charlie's initial and most popular reproduction was this wooden *nicho* with doors that could open and close. The nativity figures inside were cast of resin from Charlie's originals and then carefully painted by hand. At first the work was done in the Philippines. The workers there seemed to understand this Colonial style, perhaps because they were also colonized by Spain at one time and had also accepted Catholicism centuries ago. Eventually, the factory in the Philippines closed and the work of making the nativity reproductions was moved to China. The quality of the work suffered, and when problems of quality were mentioned, the parent company made the decision to simply stop making them. That decision was unfortunate.

Susan's Christmas Shop sold thousands of these wonderful and affordable nativities in the 1980s and 1990s. Charlie used to come to my house to sign the bottom of dozens of the wooden *nichos* that were all over my living room floor. Hundreds of customers wish they could buy them today. Charlie Carrillo still owns the original nativity he made so long ago, the prototype for the reproduction. A photo of the original can be seen in my previous book, *Nativities of the Southwest,* on page 95. Charlie hopes to create a new nativity to be reproduced, and I hope to sell it in my shop.

RETABLOS BY LYNN GARLICK (2015)

4½ in. (11½ cm.) tall

Susan's Christmas Shop, Santa Fe, New Mexico

Lynn Garlick lives in Taos, New Mexico. She paints religious images in the regional style of New Mexico *retablos,* or a flat representation of a saint. She prints these images and glues them onto lightweight wood in several sizes. Her *retablos* can be used as Christmas ornaments or be hung on a wall. More specific information about each saint is on a paper glued to the back of the *retablo.* Susan's Christmas Shop has sold these for many years, beginning in the 1980s. Among the most popular *retablos* are St. Francis of Assisi, the patron saint of Santa Fe; Our Lady of Guadalupe; and San Pasqual, the patron saint of cooks.

STERLING SILVER PINS BY CATHERINE MAZIÈRE (2015)

The silver pins are 1¼ in. (3 cm.) tall
Susan's Christmas Shop, Santa Fe, New Mexico

Catherine Mazière was born in France, but has lived in Santa Fe for many years. She has made sterling silver pins and pendants for Susan's Christmas Shop from 1995 to the present. Some of these pins represent famous historical New Mexico churches on the High Road to Taos, such as the Santuario de Chimayó and the churches at Las Trampas, Truchas, and Ranchos de Taos. Smaller pins include the silver ladder, which could suggest either a kiva ladder or the ladder in the patio at the home of Georgia O'Keeffe in Abiquiú. The gleam of silver has a perennial appeal in the Southwest, especially when fashioned in such an artistic style as Catherine's designs. Eventually, Catherine will retire to Lyon, France, where she has inherited her mother's historic house.

WHEAT STRAW APPLIQUÉ CROSSES BY CARLTON GALLEGOS (2010)

The corn cross is 8 in. (20¼ cm.) tall
Collection of the author, Santa Fe, New Mexico (center), and Susan's Christmas Shop, Santa Fe, New Mexico (left and right)

Wheat straw appliqué on wood is usually assumed to be a Spanish Colonial technique. It is sometimes called "poor man's gold" and can always be seen at Spanish Market in Santa Fe. However, a few Pueblo Indians at Santa Ana Pueblo also learned the wheat straw appliqué technique. Many years ago, when there were two very old people at Santa Ana Pueblo who knew how to do it, Carlton Gallegos taught himself the technique so it would not be lost when the old artisans died.

Carlton is a Santa Ana Pueblo farmer, and he grows corn. The cross in the center features Carlton's original corn design. It is like the prayer of a Pueblo farmer, showing everything he needs to grow corn: the sun, the rain clouds, and the growing corn. I have given this cross to several Pueblo friends, and I own this one.

Santa Ana Pueblo is a few miles west of Bernalillo. Most pueblo members live and farm in Bernalillo by the Rio Grande, where the land is more suitable for farming. The old village is preserved and kept without running water or electricity. The road to Santa Ana Pueblo is unlocked only on special feast days. Several of Carlton's wheat straw crosses hang in the recently restored adobe church at Santa Ana Pueblo. The old church is often locked after midmorning, even on a feast day, so it is difficult to see. Attending Easter Mass is recommended for those who want to step back centuries inside a Colonial adobe church.

DEER DANCER AND *PASCOLA* ORNAMENTS (1998)

The deer dancer is 5½ in. (14 cm.) tall
Collection of the author, Santa Fe, New Mexico

Yaquis are Mexican Indians. There is a Yaqui Indian village in Tucson, Arizona. This band of Indians crossed the border into the United States in the early twentieth century, when they were being persecuted by the Mexican government. Easter is one of the most important Yaqui holidays, and there is a dance in that small village on the Saturday night before Easter. This dance features several deer dancers and a *pascola,* a dancer representing an old man.

There is also a little outdoor market in the village during Easter weekend, full of various booths. One booth that I visited offered handmade ornaments that portray the deer dancer and the *pascola.* I bought several of these ornaments and offered them for sale in Susan's Christmas Shop in the late 1990s. They are simply made of paper, cloth, and beads, but they evoke the feeling and style of the serious religious dance, witnessed late at night in a humble Indian village now surrounded by the large metropolis of Tucson. The vast majority of people in Tucson are completely unaware of this village and this dance and other Yaqui Easter traditions, but this is the nature of the greater Southwest. Those who learn of the special opportunities, and where and when they occur, can be privileged to witness them.

GLASS ORNAMENTS

Susan's Christmas Shop has always offered a selection of mouth-blown, hand-painted glass ornaments. These popular Christmas decorations are made in several different countries now, but it all began in Germany in the nineteenth century.

Shiny, lightweight, glass Christmas ornaments first appeared in the 1840s in Lauscha, Germany. Glassblowing had begun in that region, the mountains of Thuringia, long before then—in 1597. The industry's original purpose was making window glass, drinking vessels, bowls, and jars for the wealthy. It took a lot of wood to heat the glass ovens, and because of this, new glassworks were illegal to build, so the glassblowers worked in their own homes as a cottage industry. They would buy clear glass tubes from the large glassworks. They used these glass tubes to blow Christmas ornaments over a Bunsen burner in their homes. Usually it was the father who blew the glass, and other family members would complete the other steps necessary to have a product to sell. In the nineteenth century, there was no one poorer than a glassblower and his family, and they worked very hard to make inexpensive glass Christmas ornaments. In the nineteenth century, F. W. Woolworth imported many glass Christmas ornaments from Germany to sell in his five-and-dime stores. Now the glass ornament makers work in modern factories, and they earn more for their skilled work, but techniques that evolved in the nineteenth century are still used today.

To make a Christmas ornament, the glassblower heats the clear glass tube over a flame till it softens. One end of the hot glass tube is pinched shut. Then the glassblower places the softened glass into a mold, places the open end of the glass tube in his or her mouth, and then blows steadily to force the softened glass into all the crevices of the mold. The clear glass shape is then set in sand to cool, and it is given a full day to rest before it is silvered.

To make a clear glass ornament become shiny and reflective, a liquid sterling silver solution is poured into the long "pike," the functional temporary handle of the ornament. A worker then holds several glass ornaments by their pikes beneath a bath of hot water, stirring them long enough for the silver solution to coat the inside evenly. Uneven silvering can show up after the ornament is painted, so the careful execution of this step is vital. The silvered glass is set aside to dry and rest for a day and a night.

A base coat on the ornament is achieved by submerging them, one at a time, into a tub of paint. Then the ornament is twirled to remove excess paint and set on large racks to dry. Finally, the prepared glass ornament reaches the hands of the skilled painters. At Inge-Glas, the best German company making glass ornaments today, a painter, usually a woman, continues to work on her ornament till it is done. She may take two to four days to complete the job. Then another worker applies glue and glitter. Finally the pike is cut off and the metal cap that allows the ornament to hang is inserted. The finished ornaments are then packed into boxes to be shipped to shops. It typically takes a week, and several different skilled workers, to make a high-quality glass ornament. At Susan's Christmas Shop, there is a huge selection of mouth-blown, hand-painted glass ornaments from which to choose. Customers are offered velvet-lined baskets to hold their choices. Eventually these glass ornaments bring pleasure to those customers as they enjoy their sparkling beauty on their own Christmas trees.

The sequence of making mouth-blown, hand-painted glass ornaments, from clear (bottom left) to painted (center).

CHRISTMAS CLOUDHOPPER BY CHRISTOPHER RADKO (1997)

10 in. (25½ cm.) tall
Collection of the author, Santa Fe, New Mexico

Christopher Radko is a talented American designer of Polish descent. When he was a very young boy, he loved his family's fourteen-foot-tall Christmas tree, decorated with over two thousand heirloom glass ornaments from three generations. In 1984, the family Christmas tree fell over, breaking many of the ornaments. To replace them, Christopher sought glassblowers in Poland, where he still had relatives. He also began to design his own mouth-blown, hand-painted Christmas ornaments. He started his company, Christopher Radko, in 1986. His designs were fresh, excellent, and innovative, extravagant in size, quality, and price, and he honored the fine ornament designers of the past. He encouraged glassblowers to recover antique molds. He sought the finest artisans available in Europe—in Poland, Germany, the Czech Republic, and Italy, countries that have a long tradition of Christmas art. He revived styles of glass ornaments made before World War II, and he created a renaissance in glass Christmas ornaments that continues to this day. Christopher eventually sold his business and is no longer designing ornaments. Susan's Christmas Shop sold Christopher Radko glass ornaments for many years, from 1986 till 2009.

This large Radko glass ornament is called "Christmas Cloudhopper." It was designed in 1997. It was mouth-blown, hand-painted, and assembled in Poland. It is a significant achievement in glassblowing. It was carefully wrapped by hand with gold wire, with a pressed papier-mâché Santa figure carefully placed inside the wires. It was originally priced at $70.00, so it was an extravagant luxury ornament. These are no longer being made today.

GLASS ANGEL BY THE DE CARLINI FAMILY (2005) / CLIP-ON BIRD FROM THE CZECH REPUBLIC (1998)

The glass angel is 8 in. (20¼ cm.) tall
Collection of the author, Santa Fe, New Mexico

Italian glass ornaments are not blown into molds like German glass ornaments. Instead, the hot molten glass is controlled with paddles. This requires a different type of skill, and results in very distinctive ornaments. Frequently, fabric costumes and accessories are added after the glass has cooled. Christopher Radko's company once sold beautiful Italian glass ornaments made by the De Carlini family in northern Italy. The De Carlini family business began in the 1950s, long before Christopher Radko began his career, and it continues to make special glass ornaments under the De Carlini family name today.

The large white clip-on bird was created with the use of a mold for the shape of the body. The long neck and open beak of the bird were fashioned with hot glass without the use of a mold. It was made in the Czech Republic in the 1990s.

GOLD FOIL ANGEL IN GLASS ORNAMENT FROM GERMANY (1980s)

$2^{1}/_{2}$ in. ($6^{1}/_{4}$ cm.) in diameter
Collection of Rich Bozanich,
Rancho Palos Verdes, California

This lovely German glass ornament is not silvered inside. Instead, an elaborately tooled gold foil angel was carefully inserted through a large hole in the bottom. The hole was then covered with an ornamental piece of gold foil. This design began in the 1960s, but is not currently being made. This was sold at Susan's Christmas Shop in the 1980s.

GLASS BEAD ORNAMENTS FROM THE CZECH REPUBLIC (2005)

The bicycle is 3 in. (7½ cm.) long
Collection of the author, Santa Fe, New Mexico (left and right), and Susan's Christmas Shop, Santa Fe, New Mexico (center)

In the 1890s, a new type of glass ornament appeared. Czechoslovakian glass bead makers created fancy shapes using short lengths of hollow glass tubing and beads strung on thin wire. This remains almost exclusively a specialty of the Czech Republic. Stars and geometric shapes were historically made with this technique, but recently, novel and creative shapes like a can of sardines, a bicycle, and a coffee grinder (left to right) have appeared. The best company for this work is Contia, and the company still makes glass bead ornaments today.

RUSSIAN JEWEL GLASS ORNAMENTS (1979)

2¼ in. (5¾ cm.) in diameter
Collection of Sylvia Hughes, Albuquerque, New Mexico

For a year or so, a special kind of glass ornament was made in Russia. They were shaped like large faceted jewels. They were silvered inside, but only on one half. That must have been tricky to achieve. Then each ornament was painted with a transparent color on the outside. These glass ornaments flashed light in a distinctive way. They were called "Russian Jewels." After the Soviet Union invaded Afghanistan in 1979, it became impossible to obtain these ornaments, and they are no longer made today. Customers who own Russian Jewels are fortunate.

PALACE OF THE GOVERNORS

PALACE OF THE GOVERNORS BY LANDMARK CREATIONS (2001)

4 in. (10 cm.) wide
Collection of the author, Santa Fe, New Mexico

Poland is currently a primary source for custom glass ornaments. Landmark Creations is one American company producing custom glass ornaments in Poland. This company has made an exclusive series of glass ornaments for Susan's Christmas Shop called "Landmarks of New Mexico," each one depicting a historical landmark. The first in the series was the Palace of the Governors, first blown into a custom mold in Poland in 2001. The Palace of the Governors is the oldest public building in the United States, built in 1610 as the official government building. It is on the Plaza, a half block east of Susan's Christmas Shop.

Other New Mexico landmarks that have inspired custom glass ornaments by Landmark Creations include the Cathedral Basilica of St. Francis of Assisi and Loretto Chapel in Santa Fe, the Santuario de Chimayó on the High Road to Taos, the San Miguel Chapel in Santa Fe, the San Felipe de Neri Church in Albuquerque, the church at Ranchos de Taos, the seventeenth-century San Esteban del Rey Mission Church at Acoma Pueblo, and the pink Scottish Rite Temple in Santa Fe.

THE SHED GLASS ORNAMENT BY ARTISTRY OF POLAND (2005)

3½ in. (9 cm.) tall
Susan's Christmas Shop, Santa Fe, New Mexico

Artistry of Poland is another American company creating mouth-blown, custom glass ornaments in Kraków, Poland. The first design was Our Lady of Guadalupe. Susan's Christmas Shop sold fifty-six dozen Our Lady of Guadalupe ornaments in 2002, the first year it was introduced. Later custom designs made by Artistry of Poland for Susan's Christmas Shop include the Santa Fe Opera, the Santuario de Guadalupe in Santa Fe, and the Pueblo pottery designs of Santo Domingo Pueblo, Zia Pueblo, and Acoma Pueblo.

The Shed glass ornament is an Artistry of Poland best seller to those who love their "Number 4." The description of this most popular menu item is on the back of this ornament, using the language on The Shed's menu. Mocha Cake is the most famous dessert. Customers at my shop can often tell you how long they have eaten at The Shed. I first ate there in 1963.

GLASS ORNAMENTS FROM MEXICO (1990s)

3 in. (7½ cm.) tall

Collection of Melissa Weber, Tucson, Arizona

Mexico has a history of blowing glass, usually producing simple dishes and drinking glasses. For a few years, unusual glass Christmas ornaments were created in Mexico. They were made with the technique of Italian glass ornaments, which is without the use of molds. The styles shown here represent a *China poblana* (the girl) and a *charro* (the boy) in their famous regional costumes of Mexico. Braid and glitter were added after the ornaments were painted. These were made in the 1990s. Unfortunately, these glass ornaments are no longer being made.

GLASS KNIGHT IN SHINING ARMOR (1997)

7½ in. (19 cm.) tall

Collection of Mr. and Mrs. Jason Trainor, Santa Fe, New Mexico

One December day in 1997, a young man named Jason Trainor came into my shop looking earnest. We asked if we could help him. "This is my favorite shop," he said. "I've been shopping here since I was a boy. My girlfriend loves Christmas too, and I want to ask her to marry me, using a Christmas ornament." We looked and looked and finally found this glass knight in shining armor. On the back of the knight, on his red cape, Jane Shea, an artist who was working at Susan's Christmas Shop that day, wrote a proposal of marriage in gold, using Jason's chosen words.

Jason hid the glass ornament on their Christmas tree. He told his girlfriend that he had not been able to afford to buy her a Christmas present that year, but only a Christmas ornament. His girlfriend had decorated the tree by herself, and was familiar with every ornament. She rushed over to the Christmas tree and looked, found the new ornament, read its proposal, and when she turned around, there were tears of joy in her eyes. She said "Yes," and they have been happily married for many years. They now have two teenaged children.

Rolyn,
Will you
marry me?
Jason
Christmas 1997

LATER ARTISTS AND ARTISANS

PAINTED GOOSE EGGS BY CAROL BOWLES (1989)

3 in. ($7\frac{1}{2}$ cm.) tall

Collection of Betty Chavez, Rio Verde, Arizona

Carol Bowles is one of those creative people who has made art since she was a child. She earned a degree in art at Penn State and later studied at the Art Institute of Chicago. She moved to Los Alamos in 1980, where she had a farm of three acres. The farm had many animals, including several geese actively laying eggs. Carol painted her original Southwest designs on the emptied goose eggshells and then strung them to hang. Originally the eggs were given as gifts, but eventually Carol sold them for her income.

Each egg had a title. These three are called "Horny Toads in Love," "*Koshari* at Santo Domingo," and "Spring Time Comes to Taos Pueblo" (left to right). *Koshari* are a kind of striped, sacred Pueblo clown seen at many New Mexico pueblos, including Santo Domingo Pueblo on August 4. They often carry boughs of evergreen and hand them to pueblo spectators watching the dance. The last time I was there, a *koshari* handed one to me. It felt like a compliment.

Carol's eggs were sold at Susan's Christmas Shop in the late 1980s and the 1990s. They were quite collectible. Eventually Carol moved east to be closer to an aging parent. She began painting in a different style, and her delightful Southwest goose eggs are no longer made.

SNOWMAN AND DOGS CROCHET ORNAMENT (1990s)

The snowman is 3 in. (7½ cm.) tall
Collection of the author,
Santa Fe, New Mexico

These miniature crochet snowman and dogs were made by hand in China and sold as a Christmas ornament in the 1990s. Susan's Christmas Shop sold this and several other appealing crochet ornaments. Unfortunately, these crochet ornaments are no longer being made, their source is forgotten, and their designer is unknown.

CARVED WOODEN ANGEL BY MELANIE KOCH (ca. 2000)

The angel is 6 in. (15¼ cm.) tall
Collection of Donna Parker, Atlanta, Georgia

Melanie Koch lived in Santa Fe in the 1990s. She made this angel from a solid piece of wood, which she beautifully carved and delicately painted. She attached a vintage piece of metal to the back for the angel's wings. This angel was made for Susan's Christmas Shop around 2000.

BEADED CHRISTMAS TREE PINS BY BILLIE TANNEN AND ROBERT NIELSEN (2015)

The tallest tree is 4 in. (10 cm.)
Susan's Christmas Shop, Santa Fe, New Mexico

Billie Tannen finished art school in New York in the late 1980s. She had played with polymer clay as a child, and she bought it again as an adult. Her sweetheart, Robert Nielsen, used the clay to make a romantic gift of beads for Billie. Soon they were married, and both of them were making beads using the ancient millefiori technique. The name literally means *thousands of flowers*. The technique is also called caning, and glass workers in Venice use this technique.

In 1993, *Vogue* magazine called Billie and Robert to ask if they would make Christmas tree pins. They began to make pins in two sizes and many colors, and for a year or two they had a booth at the craft section of the New York Gift Show. That is where I met them in the mid-1990s. They call their work Billie Beads. They add Swarovski crystals to the Christmas tree pins for extra sparkle. The result is the best-selling Christmas pins at Susan's Christmas Shop.

DOLLS BY HELMA GÖTZ (ca. 1980)

The tallest doll is 12 in. (30½ cm.)
Collection of Sylvia Hughes,
Albuquerque, New Mexico

Helma Götz was a young doll maker in Frankfurt, Germany, when she met my mother in 1960. My father was a U.S. Army officer stationed in Frankfurt, and I went to an American high school there at that time. Helma was attracted to the shape of the heads of the toddlers in my family and she began using them as her models. Once Barbie dolls were introduced, girls lost interest in Helma's classic, more innocent-style doll. Eventually Helma retired. All of her dolls that had not sold were put in boxes in her attic. Whenever I visit Helma in Frankfurt, I bring back dolls. These are some of those dolls.

PUEBLO POTTERY FIGURES BY LYNN TOLEDO (ca. 2008)

The drummer is $3^3/4$ in. ($9^1/2$ cm.) tall
Collection of the author, Santa Fe, New Mexico

Lynn Toledo is a gifted artist from a talented family at Jemez Pueblo. She attended the prestigious Institute of American Indian Arts in Santa Fe. She made several Pueblo ornaments and nativities for Susan's Christmas Shop around 2008, using traditional Jemez clay and a palette of colors she created from natural clays. The drummer ornament (left) holds a Pueblo-style drum and sings a song for the corn dancer (right) in her belted *manta* trimmed with turquoise, with her cotton under-dress showing at the hem and her *tablita* on her head. The leaping deer (center) has a necklace of *heishi* and glass beads. *Heishi* are special Pueblo beads made of shell bits that have been drilled, strung, and ground smooth. Lynn continues to create, but prefers to sell her work directly to the public rather than through shops.

NAVAJO ROADRUNNER ORNAMENTS BY CHANDLER BEGAYE (2015)

4½ in. (11½ cm.) long
Susan's Christmas Shop, Santa Fe, New Mexico

Navajo folk art is usually carved of wood and then painted. Chandler Begaye of Aneth, Utah, made these amusing painted roadrunners in high-top tennis shoes. Since the roadrunner is the state bird of New Mexico, this is a popular ornament at Susan's Christmas Shop. Its price is twice that of other painted wooden Navajo ornaments, because it is an innovative design with great appeal that involves more work to make. Nevertheless, this ornament always sells out. Ornaments like this are not made in factories, but by individual artisans in their homes. These artisans may live a great distance from Santa Fe, and may also have full-time jobs that limit when they can take a day to drive to my shop to deliver their work.

WOODEN ANGELS BY DAVID ALVAREZ (2009)

The tallest angel is 9 in. (22¾ cm.)
Collection of the author, Santa Fe, New Mexico

David Alvarez was a talented wood-carver in Santa Fe who is no longer alive. His ethnic identity was considered to be "Spanish," which in Santa Fe means "New Mexican of Spanish ancestry." David apprenticed with the famous Santa Fe Spanish folk artist Felipe Archuleta. He was married to Louise Ortega, the youngest child of Ben Ortega, another well-known local Spanish wood-carver. David borrowed some of his ideas from his father-in-law.

David's larger carved wooden sculptures are now in museum collections. He made these angels for Susan's Christmas Shop, using driftwood he and Louise collected from the shores of New Mexico lakes. Since David's death in 2010, Louise has continued to make similar angels for Susan's Christmas Shop, but she can always identify David's angels.

DRIFTWOOD NATIVITY BY LOUISE ORTEGA (2015)

The base of the nativity is 26 in. (66 cm.) long
Private collection

Louise Ortega Alvarez has used her maiden name, Ortega, since her husband, David Alvarez, died, because her father, Ben Ortega, is more well known than the Alvarez name. She makes driftwood angels, and has also developed her skill at making driftwood nativities. Because each driftwood base is unique, no two nativities are alike. This one has a donkey behind the stable, a shepherd with a staff, his flock of sheep, and the three wise men with their acorn caps. An angel is always pegged into the wood over the nativity. The angels are designed to be removable for storing or shipping. Susan's Christmas Shop sells a steady stream of driftwood angels and nativities by Louise Ortega.

TIN ANGELS BY TRUDEL GIFFORD (ca. 1991–95)

The Seraph-fin is 11 in. (28 cm.) tall
Collections of Cindy Mares, Santa Fe, New Mexico (left and right), and Trudel Gifford, Santa Fe, New Mexico (center)

Trudel Gifford is a Santa Fe artist who created many large, lighthearted tin angels in the early 1990s. She saw a little three-dimensional clay *putto* (nude baby angel) Christmas ornament, and thought of making tin versions of her own. Trudel made a sketch and started cutting tin. She called her angels "Seraphim," but if they were mermaids, she called them "Seraph-fin."

Most of her angels had humorous names. "The Last Picture Show" (center) is dated 1995, and is an amusing reference to the Yucca Drive-In on Cerrillos Road, the last drive-in theater in Santa Fe. Trudel made this male angel after learning that the drive-in would be closed, a casualty of changing times but fondly remembered by Santa Fe teenagers of long ago. The Seraph-fin is titled "Storyteller" (left) and is dated 1991. The angel with the red and green chiles is called "Some Like It Hot" (right) and is not dated, so it might be one of her very first tin angels. Trudel's sense of humor was always evident in her designs and names, and her work is very collectible.

COCHITI ORNAMENTS BY SEAN MORNINGSTAR (2012)

The painted leather kilt is 4 in. (10 cm.) long
Susan's Christmas Shop, Santa Fe, New Mexico

Sean Morningstar is from Cochiti Pueblo, which is on the Rio Grande halfway between Santa Fe and Albuquerque. Sean's Indian name translates to "Morningstar" in English, and he signs his work with a logo representing this name. That logo is visible on the leather kilt ornament (bottom). Corn dances are done at most of the Rio Grande pueblos. They involve both male and female dancers in two long lines. The women and girls wear a *tablita* on their heads, and Sean made a *tablita* ornament of painted wood with feathers attached (left). The men and boys in a corn dance line wear an elaborately embroidered kilt around their hips. Sean used thick leather to represent the kilt, and he painted the traditional embroidery onto the leather. The small ornaments that look like Pueblo pots are actually lightweight gourds, which Sean grew himself at Cochiti. The painted designs on the little gourds are traditional Cochiti Pueblo pottery designs. These ornaments are the genuine expression of the Pueblo culture, made by someone who has lived at Cochiti Pueblo all of his life.

ISLETA PUEBLO POTTERY ORNAMENTS BY MAPOO (2015)

Each disc is $2\frac{1}{2}$ in. ($6\frac{1}{4}$ cm.) in diameter
Susan's Christmas Shop, Santa Fe, New Mexico

Mapoo is an artist from Isleta Pueblo. Isleta is on the Rio Grande just south of Albuquerque. Mapoo is her Indian name; she is also known as Gertie Sanchez. She is a prize-winning potter who displays her wares at Indian Market on the plaza of Santa Fe in late August. Mapoo forms pottery Christmas ornaments out of her native clay. They are slightly curved like a small dish. Each ornament is first covered with a slip in either white or red. Both slips have mica in them, so that flecks of mica cause the ornament to sparkle. Inside each dish, Mapoo paints beautiful designs, such as the turtle, hummingbird, and dragonfly shown in these examples. Her ornaments have sold at Susan's Christmas Shop for many years. A large nativity by Mapoo appears in my earlier book, *Nativities of the Southwest,* on page 56.

FELT ORNAMENTS FROM MIDWEST OF CANNON FALLS (1992)

The fireman is 5 in. (12½ cm.) tall
Collection of Melissa Weber, Tucson, Arizona

Midwest of Cannon Falls (now known as Midwest-CBK) is a large company with showrooms at major wholesale gift shows. I have purchased at these showrooms since 1978. Midwest offered these delightful felt ornaments for a few years. Each ornament was based on an animal dressed for various occupations or activities. They had labels identifying them as "Heart Felts." The name of the talented designer is not known. Midwest-CBK has new owners and their merchandise has also changed, and Heart Felts are no longer being made. The dalmatian firefighter (left), the monkey ballerina (center), the ant Boy Scout (right), and several other styles of Heart Felts were sold at Susan's Christmas Shop in the 1990s.

PAPER SLURRY ORNAMENTS BY DEBBIE KERWICK (ca. 2000)

3 in. (7 1/2 cm.)
Collection of Sylvia Hughes, Albuquerque, New Mexico

Debbie Kerwick is a Santa Fe housewife who makes ornaments using paper slurry and molds. The result is a lightweight Christmas ornament with great detail and great appeal. The original molds of this type were sometimes used for a molded German cookie called *springerle,* and they were originally made of hand-carved wood. Today, cast molds are commercially available. These paper ornaments by Debbie were sold at Susan's Christmas Shop in the 1990s. Debbie continues to make paper ornaments, but presents them in a slightly different way. They can still be found at Susan's Christmas Shop.

FLOWER FAIRY ORNAMENTS (1990s)

3 in. (7½ cm.)
Collection of Melissa Weber, Tucson, Arizona

A talented young woman in Santa Fe made ornaments she called "Flower Fairies" in the 1990s. She used artificial flowers, wrapped wires for arms and legs, wooden beads for the heads, and colored yarns for the hair. No two "Flower Fairies" were alike, and each one had great appeal to customers. One of my customers bought seventy of them. The artist moved away from Santa Fe when her husband was transferred to another job. She stopped making these ornaments, and her name is forgotten, but her "Flower Fairies" continue to delight the customers who bought them so long ago.

MINIATURE WOOL STOCKING AND MITTENS (1995) / HANDMADE FELT SANTA ORNAMENT FROM KYRGYZSTAN (2010)

Santa is 3 in. (7½ cm.) tall
Collection of the author, Santa Fe, New Mexico

The Taos Wool Festival occurs at Kit Carson Park in Taos during the first full weekend in October. The weather is usually glorious. It was at this popular event that I met the talented knitter who had tiny knitting needles and the patience and skill to knit the miniature stocking and mittens (left). I sold them in my shop in the 1990s. The tiny stocking is made with angora yarn.

The Santa ornament (right) was made of handmade felt in Kyrgyzstan. It was purchased from an artisan who participated in the Santa Fe International Folk Art Market from about 2010 to 2012. Like many artisans in the market, she did not want to take her unsold goods back to her home country, so she wholesaled them to shops before she left Santa Fe. She has not been selected to offer her wares at the annual Santa Fe International Folk Art Market since then. Each year, new vendors are chosen for this coveted venue.

NAVAJO AND PUEBLO MOCCASIN ORNAMENTS BY LEO BENALLY AND OTHERS (ca. 1990s)

The Navajo moccasins (far left) are 2.5 in. (6¼ cm.) long
Collections of the author, Santa Fe, New Mexico (left), and Melissa Weber, Tucson, Arizona (all others)

Moccasins are a kind of leather footwear worn by Navajo, Pueblo, and Apache people of the Southwest. Anglo people can sometimes find commercial versions of moccasins. When they are made in a small size for use as a Christmas ornament, moccasins have the appeal of the miniature and the advantage of being unbreakable. During the 1990s, a rancher's wife who lived near Coyote, New Mexico, made beaded moccasin ornaments (second from left) in two sizes. Since 2005, she has retired and no longer makes them.

The Navajo moccasin ornaments (far left) are exactly like full-sized Navajo moccasins, complete with a silver button. The Navajo maker, Leo Benally, made his moccasin ornaments for several years, but now can no longer make them. Susan's Christmas Shop purchased his final batch of moccasin ornaments.

The tiny white leather moccasins (third from left) are made of thin deerskin in a style seen at Taos Pueblo. The other two styles of moccasins are worn by Pueblo women, one with wraps of leather rising to the knees (far right). All these miniature moccasins are appropriate for a Christmas tree with a Southwest theme of decoration.

NAVAJO RUG ORNAMENTS BY LORRAINE MARK (2015) / NAVAJO FABRIC DOLL ORNAMENTS BY SYLVIA BEGAYE (2015)

The Navajo rugs are 3 in. (7½ cm.) long
Susan's Christmas Shop, Santa Fe, New Mexico

Navajo weavers are famous for their hand-woven rugs. These rugs are made with wool from the sheep of the flocks they tend. Lorraine Mark is an elderly Navajo weaver living in the Teec Nos Pos area of the Navajo Nation Reservation in Arizona. This is close to the Four Corners region, the only place in the United States where four states, Utah, Colorado, Arizona, and New Mexico, touch each other. For twenty years, Lorraine has woven miniature Navajo rugs (front) and sold them to the local trading post as key chains. These are popular as ornaments at Susan's Christmas Shop, where we remove the metal key chain ring. In her weaving, Lorraine uses traditional Navajo rug designs, but she also weaves several rugs with Christmas designs, such as a Santa, a Christmas tree, and a snowman. These are nice on Southwest Christmas trees.

Sylvia Begaye is a talented Navajo artist from Fort Defiance, Arizona. She makes small fabric doll ornaments that represent the Navajo styles of dress, hair, and jewelry. Sometimes wooden cradleboards hold their babies. The ones with cradleboards are called "Madonna and Child" (back left). Those with grey hair are called "Grandmothers" (back right). Sylvia's faces always look like Navajo faces. Her delicate piped-on jewelry looks like the real silver and turquoise jewelry the Navajo jewelers make to sell and wear themselves. These ornaments have been sold for many years at Susan's Christmas Shop, as well as Sylvia's wreaths, velvet angels, and Navajo-style Santa ornaments.

SZOPKA KRAKÓWSKA FROM POLAND (2005) / WOODEN SOLDIERS FROM CZECHOSLOVAKIA (1982)

The soldiers are 6¼ in. (16 cm.) tall
Collection of the author, Santa Fe, New Mexico

In Kraków, Poland, there is a famous fortified architectural complex called Wawel on the bank of the Vistula River. It has many distinctive buildings dating back many centuries, including the well-loved Wawel Cathedral and Wawel Castle. These two buildings, with their many towers, have inspired a contest each Christmas for the best replica, called a *szopka Krakówska,* or Kraków nativity. The custom of making *szopkę* began in the nineteenth century in Kraków. The replicas are actually composites of the cathedral and other historic architecture of Wawel, and they always are the setting for a small nativity. Several large wooden *szopkę,* collected by Alexander Girard years ago, are now in the Girard Wing of the Museum of International Folk Art in Santa Fe. Most often, these replicas are made of cardboard covered with foil, and feature towers, turrets, and foil flags flying in the breeze. Over the many years I have had my shop, I have been able to get only a few of these to sell.

This *szopka Krakówska* came from Suzanne Myal of Artistry of Poland, a company that makes custom glass ornaments for my shop. The nativity figures at the bottom level are easily overlooked because of the splendor above them. I kept this replica for my own enjoyment. It has the Polish eagle as its crowning decoration. It looks like a castle, suitable to be officially guarded by soldiers in uniforms with drawn swords. I added two wooden soldiers from Czechoslovakia that I had for sale at Susan's Christmas Shop in the 1980s. They are made of lathe-turned wood, similar to the work from the Erzgebirge across the border in Germany. The Czech soldiers are available at the present time, and occasionally I find a *szopka Krakówska* when collectors sell their collections.

REPRODUCTION OF SAN RAFAEL *BULTO* (2007)

13 in. (33 cm.) tall
Collection of the author, Santa Fe, New Mexico

The Museum of Spanish Colonial Art in Santa Fe has a famous New Mexico colonial *bulto* (carved statue) of the archangel San Rafael by José Aragón. It was made in the early nineteenth century. It is recognizable as San Rafael because he holds a fish suspended from one hand. He wears the attire of colonial angels seen all over Spain's colonial empire, but in this case interpreted in a regional New Mexican style.

A wood-carver in Los Alamos made a replica of the historic statue in a smaller size. In 2007, the smaller *bulto* was reproduced in China and sold in the gift shop of the Museum of Spanish Colonial Art. A thousand of these distinctive statues were made, beautifully molded of epoxy and splendidly painted. Susan's Christmas Shop purchased them wholesale from the Museum of Spanish Colonial Art and sold many of them in the shop for several years. Now the first edition of the San Rafael reproduction is sold out and the Museum of Spanish Colonial Art seems reluctant to make this remarkable reproduction again.

CHILE CANDLES BY ELKE STUART (2015)

8 in. (20 1/4 cm.) tall
Susan's Christmas Shop, Santa Fe, New Mexico

Elke Stuart was born and raised in Santa Fe. When she was a young girl, she loved a boutique in downtown Santa Fe called Sign of the Pampered Maiden—especially its name. Elke eventually married and moved to Southern California. A few years ago she began to sell candles she had decorated. She called her business The Pampered Maiden. I've known Elke and her family since she was a girl living in Santa Fe. Her candles are as nice as Elke herself. She decorates candles for different seasons, such as Valentine's Day, Easter, and Christmas (and my shop changes its merchandise for all these holidays). Elke's red and green chile candles are popular year-round, and a basket of her beautiful candles is always seen at Susan's Christmas Shop.

MINIATURE LEATHER AND FLEECE VICUÑA REPLICAS FROM PERU (2015)

The tallest vicuña is 3 in. (7½ cm.) tall
Collection of Melissa Weber, Tucson, Arizona (center), and Susan's Christmas Shop, Santa Fe, New Mexico (left and right)

In Peru there are the famous animals of the high Andes: the llama, the alpaca, and the vicuña. The vicuñas have the softest wool of them all, and they are protected animals. I saw these miniature vicuña replicas at the booth of a Peruvian importer at the California Gift Show. They are made of leather and fleece. At the time I first saw them, they were not intended to be ornaments. I recognized that they could become ornaments after a curved needle pierced the leather to add a loop of red string. Credit for this idea belongs to the proprietor of a famous Christmas shop in San Francisco. I never met him, nor do I know his name. And I never visited his shop, which closed long ago, but I once read that he frequently made ornaments of things he discovered. It is true that almost anything can become a Christmas ornament. It is also true that one generation can inspire another.

Lots of careful handwork went into making these charming Andean animals. Children often choose them when selecting an ornament because they are so appealing. These have been sold at Susan's Christmas Shop since 2005.

CARVED WOODEN FISH AND BIRD BY MANUEL MONTOYA (2015)

3 in. (7½ cm.) long

Susan's Christmas Shop, Santa Fe, New Mexico

Manuel Montoya is a young New Mexican Spanish wood-carver who lives in the small mountain village of Vadito, which is north of Las Trampas on the High Road to Taos. I first saw his work at a little shop close to the church at Las Trampas. Manuel's style of chip carving is similar to the famous carving done at Cordova, another village in northern New Mexico. Manuel signs his full name on each bird or fish ornament. When I want more, I write him a letter, because he has no telephone. In a few days he appears at my shop with his carefully carved work in a charming regional style. Susan's Christmas Shop has sold Manuel's work since the 1990s.

CARVED AND PAINTED HOPI *KACHINA* ORNAMENTS BY T. C. POCHOEMA (2014)

The Sun *kachina* (center) is 3 in. (7½ cm.) tall
Collections of the author, Santa Fe, New Mexico (left), and Karen Sears, Santa Fe, New Mexico (center and right)

T. C. Pochoema was born at one of the Hopi villages in northern Arizona, but he now lives in Santa Fe and has relatives at Taos Pueblo. He is talented in many ways. Susan's Christmas Shop sells his small hanging *kachina* ornaments. First he carves them and then he paints them. They have the look of vintage *kachinas,* and they are a good size to hang on a small tabletop tree with a Southwest theme. Each of these *kachinas* has a name: "Corn Maiden" (left), "Sun" (center), and "Eagle" (right).

SOUTHWEST CHURCH SCALE MODELS BY CAROLYN JOHNSON (2015)

A typical model is 2 in. (5 cm.) tall
Susan's Christmas Shop, Santa Fe, New Mexico

Carolyn Johnson has been making small, detailed models of Southwest churches since 1981. These models have just become better and more detailed as the years have passed. Carolyn now makes over fifty different churches and continues to make new ones from time to time. Her church models can hang as Christmas ornaments or sit on a shelf. Carolyn began selling her work to Susan's Christmas Shop in 1991. There are two wooden shelves on the south adobe wall of my shop, by the front door. Each shelf has dozens of small square openings, each opening the right size to hold a church model. On the bottom of each church model is a paper with information about that church. Most of the churches are located in New Mexico, but a few are in Texas. The most popular church models are the ones shown here: the Cathedral Basilica of St. Francis of Assisi in Santa Fe (center), the Loretto Chapel in Santa Fe (right), and the Santuario de Chimayó (left), a beloved pilgrim's destination on the High Road to Taos.

SANTA CHILE ORNAMENTS BY MELISSA WEBER (2015)

The tallest Santa chile is 5 in. ($12^1/_2$ cm.)
Susan's Christmas Shop, Santa Fe,
New Mexico

Red chiles are an essential part of New Mexico culture and cuisine. Hatch, New Mexico, just north of Las Cruces, is famous for growing chiles. Chiles are usually picked while they are still green. At the end of summer, Hatch green chiles can be seen being roasted outside along the side of the road or by grocery stores. If Hatch chiles are not roasted when they are green, they will turn red naturally. Red chiles are often strung up as *ristras* as a way of preserving the crop. Courtney Carswell, the owner of The Shed restaurant behind Susan's Christmas Shop, buys the entire crop of one Hatch farmer every year. He grinds these dried red chiles every day to make the delicious and addicting red sauce for his famous "Number 4" enchilada. My daughter, Melissa Weber, uses dried Hatch chiles also, but she paints sweet little Santa faces on them and strings them to hang as Christmas ornaments. They are the most popular ornaments at Susan's Christmas Shop.

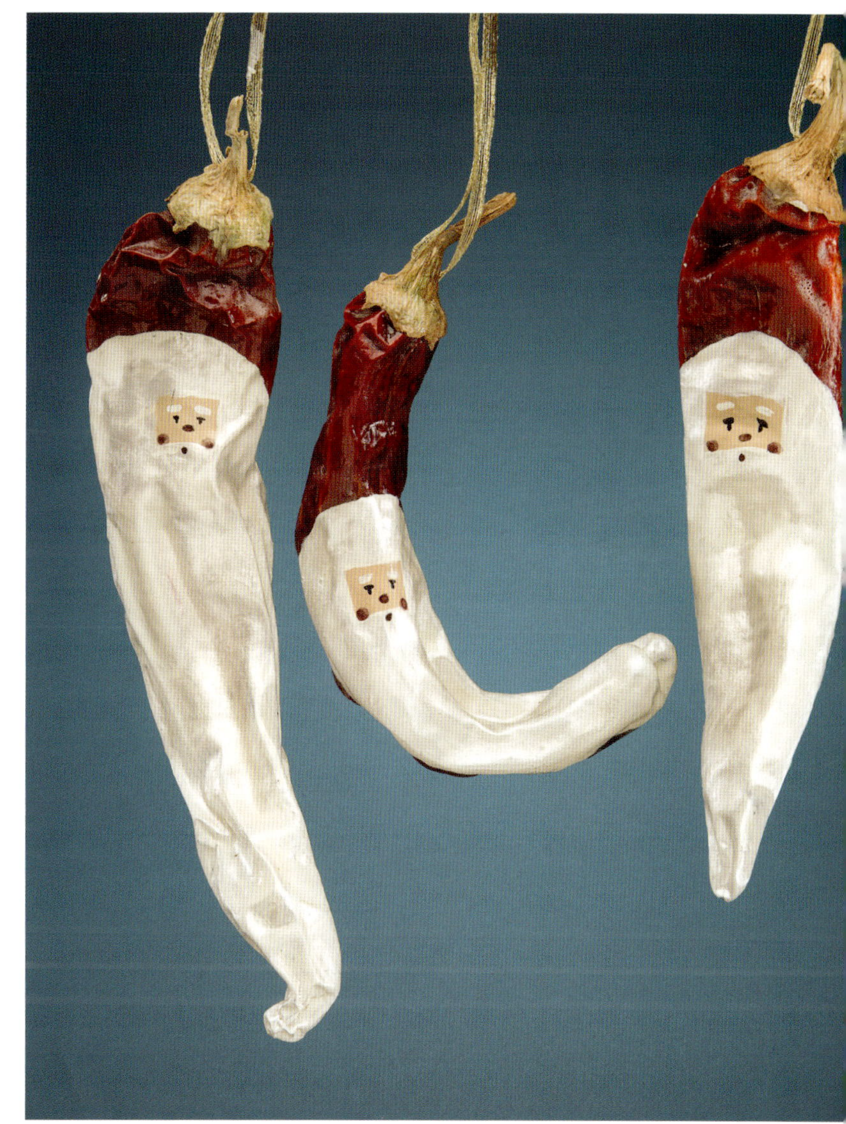

PUFFY SANTA ORNAMENTS BY KATHY PHELAN (1990s)

3 in. (7½ cm.) tall
Collections of Ellen Sierocinski, Albuquerque, New Mexico (left), and the author, Santa Fe, New Mexico (right)

Kathy Phelan is one of the most talented artists I have known. I met her in Tucson, Arizona, in 1983, when I opened a second Susan's Christmas Shop. That shop lasted only a few years. It closed and I moved back to Santa Fe, where I belong. In Tucson, Kathy was just beginning to explore a new medium, papier-mâché, which can take humble materials like tissue paper, wire, and glue and create something new and magical. One of the first things she showed me was a pinecone elf. I recognized Kathy's talent and fell in love with the elf, which I kept for myself and have cherished each Christmas since. I encouraged Kathy to make more. Her talent flowered from 1983 till she stopped making them in 1997 to care for an aging parent in another state.

Kathy made many decorations out of papier-mâché, including Halloween witches, howling coyotes, lizards, penguins dressed in red winter hats, Sugarplum Fairies, snowmen, and saguaro cactus ornaments. She called her work "Paper Dreams." One of my personal favorite ornaments by Kathy are these puffy Santa ornaments, which seem to be jumping for joy.

PAPIER-MÂCHÉ ELVES BY KATHY PHELAN (1990s)

The pinecone inspector is 3½ in. (9 cm.) tall
Collections of Ellen Sierocinski Albuquerque, New Mexico (left and right), and Kathy Phelan, Tucson, Arizona (center)

Among Kathy Phelan's most popular pieces in Susan's Christmas Shop were her red and green elves getting ready for Christmas. A couple of working elves are shown here, along with a sleeping elf. One elf is a pinecone inspector. The other elf has a list of the good boys and girls.

There were many more elves designed by Kathy, far more than could be shown here. It was a dilemma to choose which Paper Dreams would be included in this book. Kathy's first pinecone elf is not shown, and even though Kathy considers it amateur and embarrassing, it is still one of my favorite Christmas decorations. That is the heart of Kathy's talent: the unusual ability to breathe life into her creations so that her fans beg for more. All of her fans, including me, hope she will make Paper Dreams again.

PAPIER-MÂCHÉ SCENE INSPIRED BY *THE NUTCRACKER* BY KATHY PHELAN (1990s)

Herr Drosselmeyer is 3 in. ($7\frac{1}{2}$ cm.) tall
Private collection

A patron commissioned Kathy Phelan to make elaborate papier-mâché scenes in her home for every season of the year. Undoubtedly this patron has Kathy's finest work. Kathy created a major Christmas scene with the theme of *The Nutcracker* ballet. Here is Herr Drosselmeyer reading a story to the Mouse King and a Sugarplum Fairy. Don't you wish you could hear that story?

BEADED SANTA AND SNOWMAN EARRINGS AND SANTA PIN BY MELISSA WEBER (2015)

The Santa earrings are 2 in. (5 cm.) long
Susan's Christmas Shop, Santa Fe, New Mexico

In addition to making the Santa chile ornaments for my shop, my daughter, Melissa Weber, also makes beaded Santa and snowman earrings, and a beaded Santa pin. This jewelry is fun to wear at a Christmas party, and it always sells at Susan's Christmas Shop.

TRAY OF MINIATURE FRUITS, VEGETABLES, BREADS, AND CAKES (2013)

The metal baskets are 3 in. ($7\frac{1}{2}$ cm.) long
Susan's Christmas Shop, Santa Fe, New Mexico

These detailed, handmade miniature fruits, vegetables, breads, and cakes are fascinating to my customers. I first saw them many years ago at the California Gift Show in Los Angeles, and I ordered them for my shop. Little girls and boys like them. People with dollhouses like them. Vegetarians like them. Cooks like them. They are a staple in my shop, filling little baskets lined up on the counter beneath the window. Then, unexpectedly, my importer announced that they would no longer be selling them. I ordered a large quantity, a quantity that will last for a few years. When I found a supply of small, rectangular metal baskets, I hired Jessie, a seven-year-old boy, to organize the fruits and vegetables in them. He was paid for his work. It was Jessie's first job. From time to time, Jessie checks the display to make sure it is still organized.

HUMMINGBIRD ORNAMENTS (2015)

The beaded hummingbird has a wingspan of 5 in. (12½ cm.)
Susan's Christmas Shop, Santa Fe, New Mexico

Hummingbirds seem to be loved by everyone who has seen them. At Susan's Christmas Shop, there is a small white Christmas tree loaded with hummingbird ornaments. The most popular hummingbird ornament by far is the beaded one (left). Maya Indian women in Guatemala make beaded hummingbirds with glass beads in a variety of colors for a very reasonable price.

Mary Gutierrez lives in Corrales, New Mexico, a historic village just north of Albuquerque on the west side of the Rio Grande. She learned glasswork from her brother in the mid-1980s. He eventually became a priest and serves in Santa Fe, and Mary continues to work with glass. Mary's colorful glass hummingbird ornaments (right) are very popular, the second-most popular style of hummingbird at Susan's Christmas Shop.

Chinese artisans long ago invented the technique called cloisonné. Thin strips of wire form walls for enamel to be inserted and melted. The hummingbirds made with this technique (center) are colorful, lightweight, affordable decorations. The cloisonné hummingbird ornaments are also very popular in my shop, and are even purchased by customers who usually avoid Chinese work on principle.

Fritz and Gretl stood frozen with fear in the great hall of the fortress.
"Who are you, and what do you want?" asked the Winter King in a rumbling voice. His breath shot over them like an icy north wind. Fritz and Gretl trembled and could not say a word. Then Fritz thought of the loving, tired eyes of his father and drew up his courage.
"Winter King," he said, "my name is Fritz, and this is my sister, Gretl. We beg you with all our hearts to give us one of your white winter roses. Our father is ill and can only be cured by your flower. Please help us."
Gretl took a step forward, held out her hands, and cried out in a voice choked with tears, "Please . . . please!" She was unable to say anything more.
The Winter King remained motionless. Then he nodded and ordered, "Bring a flower!"
A little mouse soon scurried in, carrying a winter rose. The On the slender stem hung an unscented white bud. The flower had not yet bloomed.
DECEMBER 15
15

PAGES FROM *THE CHRISTMAS ROSE* BY SEPP BAUER, WITH ILLUSTRATIONS BY ELSE WENZ-VIËTOR, PUBLISHED BY CHARLESBRIDGE (2008)

The book is 48 pages, hardcover, 6¾ x 9 in. (17 x 23 cm.)
Collection of the author, Santa Fe, New Mexico

In 1920, a delightful children's book was published in Germany as a kind of advent calendar. The title of the book in English is *The Christmas Rose.* Advent calendars are a German tradition intended for young children, to help them endure the long wait till Christmas Day. Each day of December the child gets to open a cardboard door, usually on a paper calendar. Inside there might be a pretty picture or a piece of chocolate. Today most advent calendars are large, flat pictures and usually begin on December 1, but in the early twentieth century some advent calendars began on December 6 because that is St. Nicholas Day. *The Christmas Rose* begins on December 6. This book was written as a story, and one page of the story is read each day. By Christmas Day, the story is completed and Christmas has arrived.

A self-taught artist, Else Wenz-Viëtor lived from 1882 till 1973. During the 1920s and 1930s, she was a prolific and well-known illustrator in Germany. Else created the illustrations for *The Christmas Rose.* In the original German edition, they were printed in color on white paper, cut out, and glued down on the cardboard on which the text was printed. The author of *The Christmas Rose* is Sepp Bauer. It is a nice story, but Else's illustrations are what make the book so wonderful. After its initial publication, *The Christmas Rose* went out of print and was all but forgotten. Else's original illustrations were probably destroyed during World War II. Many years later, one of Else's daughters told a German editor about the book, but she didn't have a copy. The editor began searching though used bookstores. Finally he found a copy in an antiquarian bookshop in Switzerland in 2006. *The Christmas Rose* was reprinted in German the same year, and in 2008 the first English edition was published. The English edition has a red ribbon bookmark, so that the correct numbered page in the story can be found each day. Each day has a beautiful color illustration by Else. I sold this remarkable Christmas book in my shop for a year or two, but it is now out of print. This book is special. Some of my customers would buy a stack of the books. I hope it is reprinted again.

MAJOLICA SANTA RIDING A POLAR BEAR BY NATALIA PAVLOVA (2015)

4½ in. (11½ cm.) tall
Susan's Christmas Shop, Santa Fe, New Mexico

Majolica is a tin-oxide glaze used on terra-cotta pottery. It originated in the Middle East centuries ago, and was brought to Spain by the Moors. Early majolica tiles can be seen in the Hispanic Society of America museum in New York City. From Spain, majolica spread to many European countries and to Mexico. Delft is a kind of majolica, as is the pottery from Puebla, Mexico. This majolica is from Russia. Santa is riding a friendly polar bear, holding a happy child in front of him. It has been hand painted. The designer is Natalia Pavlova, who also designs many majolica ornaments. These have been sold at Susan's Christmas Shop from 2000 to the present.

COVER OF *GUSTAVE BAUMANN AND FRIENDS* BY JEAN MOSS AND THOMAS LEECH, PUBLISHED BY MUSEUM OF NEW MEXICO PRESS (2014) / REPRINTED CHRISTMAS CARD BY GUSTAVE BAUMANN (1992)

The book is 116 pages, 9¼ in. (23½ cm.) tall; the card box is 7¼ in. (18½ cm.) wide
Collection of the author, Santa Fe, New Mexico

Gustave Baumann's name is well known in Santa Fe. He lived in Santa Fe for most of his long life, but he was born in Germany in 1881. He moved with his family to Chicago when he was a ten-year-old boy. He left high school to pursue a career in art and printing. He spent time back in Munich, Germany, studying art and wood-block printing. Baumann then returned to Chicago, where he created colored wood-block prints. He also spent time in an artist colony in Brown County, Indiana. Baumann loved Christmas, and before he moved west to Santa Fe, he was already sending Christmas cards he had made with carved wood-blocks. Some of these original Baumann Christmas cards are now in the collection of the Art Institute of Chicago.

Baumann arrived in Santa Fe in 1918. Within a few years he had married Jane Devereux Henderson, an actress and opera singer. They had one child, a daughter named Ann. Santa Fe was a much smaller town then, and included an active artist colony. The Baumanns probably knew every artist in town. These artistic people delighted in making handmade Christmas cards to send to each other. Gustave and Jane Baumann saved every one of these cards. Eventually, Ann gave the entire collection of artists' Christmas cards to the New Mexico History Museum. The result of this gift was a wonderful exhibit of the handmade cards at the museum, and a book about the cards by Jean Moss and Thomas Leech. The Museum of New Mexico Press published *Gustave Baumann and Friends* in 2014. This book is enormously popular in Santa Fe. I ordered it for my shop and I still sell it, autographed by both the authors.

In 1992, Gallison Books wholesaled boxes of a Christmas card originally designed by Gustave Baumann in 1916 to send to his friends. The original Baumann card is now in the collection of the Art Institute of Chicago. I sold the reprinted Baumann card in my shop in 1992. I liked the style and the sentiment. The style of the card is unmistakably Baumann's, but it predates his move to Santa Fe. It has the look of rural Indiana, reminding me of summer visits to country cousins in Indiana as a child. I kept the sturdy box the cards came in.

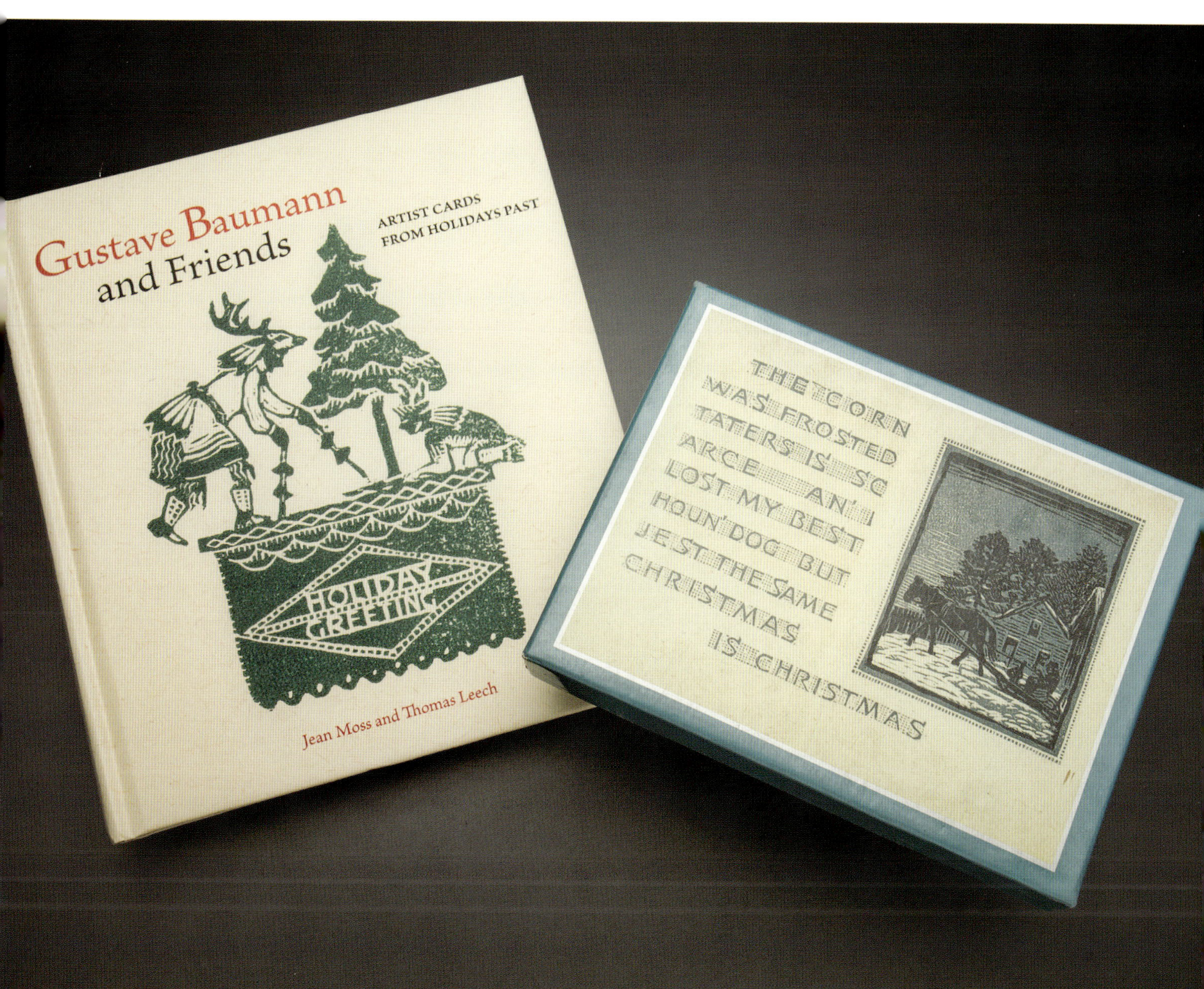
Gustave Baumann
and Friends
ARTIST CARDS
FROM HOLIDAYS PAST
HOLIDAY
GREETING
Jean Moss and Thomas Leech
THE CORN
WAS FROSTED
TATERS IS SC
ARCE AN' I
LOST MY BEST
HOUN' DOG BUT
JEST THE SAME
CHRISTMAS
IS CHRISTMAS

SANTA SNOW GLOBE (2015)

4 in. (10 cm.) tall
Susan's Christmas Shop, Santa Fe, New Mexico

Snow globes offer a snowy scene inside a clear glass ball. The glass ball is filled with liquid and placed on a base. When the base is lifted and turned over it begins to snow in the magic realm inside the glass. The best snow globes are made in Vienna, Austria. This is the type that's been sold at Susan's Christmas Shop for over thirty years.

Kathy Chilton lives in the North Valley area of Albuquerque, New Mexico. Her skill for mending and restoring almost anything has made her invaluable to my shop for decades. When I am in Albuquerque, I frequently stop by her house to drop off items that need her help, or to pick up items that she has repaired. Over the years, Kathy has often had foreign guests living at her house for a period of time.

One year, Kathy had a man from Nepal living with her family in December. He was a poor man who had nothing. It was December 5, the eve of St. Nicholas Day. It is a Chilton family tradition that everyone in the house hang a stocking that night, and in that stocking each family member places a letter to Santa, to tell him what to bring for Christmas that year. Kathy and her husband wondered what the man from Nepal would ask for. He had never heard of Christmas or Santa before. When everyone else had gone to bed, they read his letter. He had written, "Dear Santa, I would like you to bring me a picture of yourself inside a glass ball, so that I can take it back to Nepal to show my family."

Kathy decided that he was asking for a snow globe. She looked everywhere for a snow globe with a Santa inside, but she could not find one. She gave up and bought him a practical gift instead. On Christmas Eve that year, there was a Christmas Eve dinner, another Chilton family tradition. At that dinner, some close family friends were always invited, and every year they brought a little gift for each family member. That year they brought an extra gift for the man from Nepal. The wife said to Kathy in the kitchen, "I don't know what he'll do with it, and it's a bit heavy, but this is what I bought for him." It was a snow globe with a Santa inside. Kathy says she now believes in Santa.

RECYCLED TIN ORNAMENTS BY KATHY O'NEILL (2015)

The Our Lady of Guadalupe shrine is 8½ in. (21½ cm.) tall
Susan's Christmas Shop, Santa Fe, New Mexico

Kathy O'Neill lives in the countryside close to Glorieta, New Mexico, east of Santa Fe. Like several other artists who make things for Susan's Christmas Shop, Kathy has a degree in art. She creates unique and stylish items out of recycled tin and other materials. Her larger pieces include mirror frames and lampshades. For Susan's Christmas Shop, Kathy makes ornaments and shrines. Flattened bottle caps are featured in her ornament designs (right). Flowers and petals are often glued onto the shrines. Each shrine is unique, but the theme of Our Lady of Guadalupe (center) is a perennial favorite.

MOOSE FELT ORNAMENT FROM MIDWEST OF CANNON FALLS (1995) / FOX AND MOUSE FELT ORNAMENTS FROM ROOST (2015)

The moose is 6 in. (15 1/4 cm.) tall
Collection of the author, Santa Fe, New Mexico (center), and
Susan's Christmas Shop, Santa Fe, New Mexico (left and right)

These little hikers are ornaments that Susan's Christmas Shop has sold over the years. The moose with the corduroy pants and green sweater is one of the delightful Heart Felt ornaments once offered by Midwest of Cannon Falls in the 1990s. The fox and traveling mouse are newer designs from an innovative company called Roost. Customers of Susan's Christmas Shop are always hoping to find handmade ornaments like these. Because they are not breakable, they will likely survive if they are given to a child, and they always make people smile.

MOTHER AND BABY DOUGH ORNAMENT BY VANNI LOWDENSLAGER (1998)

4 in. (10 cm.) tall

Collection of Melissa Weber, Tucson, Arizona

Vanni Lowdenslager is always innovating new techniques and new designs. Her first dough ornaments (page 54) were flat. Next Vanni tried small solid figures (page 63). In an attempt to create a larger figure, and at the same time avoid a thick and heavy ornament more likely to crack, Vanni curled an incised sheet of dough. It has the shape of a cone and looks three-dimensional, but it is lighter. The hand-stamped designs on the dress are feminine and lacy, perfect for the maternal theme of the ornament. The dainty new mother proudly holds her precious baby boy. The baby is a separate piece, attached to his mother's arms. Vanni made very few ornaments of this design. When I saw it, I chose it to give to my daughter, who had just borne a son. Later Vanni abandoned this round design in favor of larger flat ornaments, incised and painted on both sides (page 157).

SOUTHWEST GOOSE EGG *PYSANKA* BY SUSAN SUMMERS (2015)

3½ in. (9 cm.) tall
Private collection

Ukrainian Easter eggs are called *pysanky*. Susan Summers first witnessed *pysanky* being made at the annual demonstrations of the craft sponsored by Susan's Easter Shop during Lent. The technique of making *pysanky* is ancient, going back at least two thousand years in the Ukraine. It involves fresh whole eggs, a cake of pure beeswax, a lit candle or heat source to melt the beeswax, handled tools called *kistky* to hold the melted beeswax as a pen would hold ink, and jars of brilliant dyes. Susan knew instantly when she first touched a *kistka* that she had to make *pysanky*. After more than twenty-five years of practice, she is at an expert level very few reach. Susan's eggs take eight to ten hours of her expert skill. Susan uses many elaborate traditional Ukrainian designs on her *pysanky*, but she also uses Southwest designs, which makes her work unique. This goose egg has a Navajo Ye'ii Bicheii design. It is the most popular of Susan's many Southwest designs for *pysanky*.

FELT ORNAMENTS BY LEAH KOSTOPLOS (2015)

The girl (right) is 8 in. (20¼ cm.) tall
Private collection

Leah Kostoplos is a Santa Fe artist who designs and makes wonderful felt Christmas ornaments. Leah has a degree in art from the Herron School of Art in Indiana. She moved to Ranchos de Taos, New Mexico, in 2005. She first sold her felt ornaments in Taos, and then to Susan's Christmas Shop in Santa Fe. Eventually she moved to Santa Fe, and now works part-time at Susan's Christmas Shop. In only a few years, Leah has acquired a growing number of collectors who love her work. She uses the finest felt available, and her original designs are enchanting. Leah's talent is exceeded only by her modesty, and she does not announce to customers that she is the artist who made what they are buying. The Mexican boy and girl ornaments are holding calla lilies.

CUSTOM FELT ORNAMENT BY LEAH KOSTOPLOS (2010)

7 in. (17 3/4 cm.) tall

Collection of the author, Santa Fe, New Mexico

The famous Matachines dance is held at Jemez Pueblo on December 12, where no photography is allowed. It has long been my favorite version of the dance, and on December 12, Our Lady of Guadalupe Day, I am usually at Jemez Pueblo to watch it. In May 2008, the first gathering of Matachines dance groups was held at the National Hispanic Cultural Center in Albuquerque. The Jemez dance group was one of eleven Southwest Matachines groups from Spanish villages, New Mexico pueblos, and a Tarajumara village from northern Mexico invited to participate over a span of two days. Each group was asked if photography of their dance was allowed. To my surprise, the Jemez Matachines group allowed photography. That set a precedent, at least for that venue. Ann Murdy, a Santa Fe photographer and big fan of Matachines, was there with her camera. The photos she took that day are on pages 76 to 79 of my first book, *Christmas in Santa Fe.*

The following year, the Jemez Matachines group again danced at the National Hispanic Cultural Center, and again they allowed photography. Again, Ann Murdy was there with her camera. I was sitting in my chair, minding my own business and enjoying the dance, when an assistant *abuelo* came over to me, took my hand, and pulled me out of my chair to dance. His grandmother, Bernice Gauchupin, had told him to do this in order to make people laugh. Making people laugh is part of the job of assistant *abuelos.* Indeed, people laughed. I showed Leah Kostoplos the picture Ann had taken of me dancing with the assistant *abuelo,* and Leah made this felt ornament for me as a gift.

PUNCHED-TIN TREE TOP AND ORNAMENTS BY BC DESIGNS (2015)

The star tree top is 10 in. (25½ cm.) tall
Susan's Christmas Shop, Santa Fe, New Mexico

Punched tin has a long history in New Mexican crafts, dating back to the territorial days when canned goods were first available. The cans were sometimes flattened and used to make decorative frames for mirrors and crosses. BC Designs is an innovative New Mexican design team making unpainted punched-tin items. Their studio is located in South Valley, near Albuquerque, New Mexico. They use tin in sophisticated ways for home décor and Christmas ornaments. Their original designs are found at the Spanish Markets in Santa Fe in July and in Albuquerque in November. The punched-tin star tree top (center) can stand by itself or go on a tree. The twisted icicles (bottom) catch the light when they are hanging on a Christmas tree. Susan's Christmas Shop offers tree tops and several tin ornament styles by BC Designs.

TIN SHED DOOR ORNAMENT BY NOEL CHILTON (2008)

5 in. (12 1/2 cm.) tall
Susan's Christmas Shop, Santa Fe, New Mexico

The Shed restaurant behind Susan's Christmas Shop is so beloved that many customers are interested in handmade ornaments to remind them of the meals they have enjoyed there over the years. I asked Kathy Chilton's daughter, Noel, to design this tin ornament of the front door of The Shed. Noel was living in Oaxaca, Mexico, at the time, where many Mexican tin ornaments are crafted. She knew the best tinsmith in Oaxaca personally. Noel has since moved back to Albuquerque, but we occasionally are able to get this custom ornament from Oaxaca. Unlike the custom glass Shed ornament (page 90), this one will not break.

EMBROIDERED HEART ORNAMENTS BY BRENDA MARES (2015)

Each embroidered heart is 3 in. (7½ cm.) wide
Susan's Christmas Shop, Santa Fe, New Mexico

Brenda Mares lives in Santa Fe. Her mother, Cindy Mares, has a large collection of embroidered pieces by the late Ann Spiess Mills. Ann Mills lived in Santa Fe from the 1950s to the 1990s, supporting herself with her embroidery. Ann's work was sold at Suzette's, a French boutique at the La Fonda. Brenda was inspired by Ann's distinctive style of embroidery, and began to copy hearts from her mother's collection. Women and needlework seem to go together. Two female collectors plan to write a book about Ann Mills. Susan's Christmas Shop now offers Brenda's embroidered heart ornaments, which combine fine handwork with a symbol of love and an homage to Ann Spiess Mills.

DOUGH ORNAMENTS BY VANNI LOWDENSLAGER (2014)

The boy ornament is 4 in. (10 cm.) tall
Susan's Christmas Shop, Santa Fe, New Mexico

Vanni Lowdenslager has changed the style of her work over the many years since she made the first ornaments seen on page 54. She now designs custom cookie cutters. Because her dough shrinks so much, the cookie cutters are larger than the finished ornaments. By making thinner ornaments, Vanni avoids the risk of cracks developing, and she can use her many assorted tools to embellish the dough on both sides. When the ornament is completely dry, Vanni paints both sides. Her faces are drawn by hand. This boy and girl were made with the use of Vanni's specially designed cookie cutters. Vanni has a few collectors who long for her earlier styles of pure white angels or adorable mice with whiskers, but her increasing age (she is now in her 80s) and the gradual deterioration of her eyesight are reminders that she cannot go back. Instead, new collectors are attracted to her current style. Susan's Christmas Shop is fortunate to have carried Vanni's work for so many years.

PAINTED EGG GOURDS BY FRANCES MANN (2015)

Koshari (center) is 4 in. (10 cm.) wide and 3 in. (7½ cm.) tall
Private collections

Frances Mann lives in Corrales, a very old community on the west side of the Rio Grande just north of Albuquerque. Around 2005, she began to paint large gourds. Then she saw egg gourds at a meeting of a local gourd society. Egg gourds are the size and shape of an egg. Frances obtained seeds and planted her own egg gourds. When the gourds are harvested, they must dry for a year. Smaller egg gourds are quite sturdy and ideal for use as Christmas ornaments. Frances turns them into works of art, using books about *kachinas* and her imagination. Her feather choices are stunning and she occasionally adds tiny shells, corn husks, and other embellishments. Each gourd has a title, such as "Snake Dancer" (left), "*Koshari*" (center), and "Parrot *Kachina*" (right). *Koshari* are striped Pueblo clowns seen at the Rio Grande pueblos during corn dances. The snake dancer from Hopi pueblos in Arizona holds a live rattlesnake in his mouth as he dances. Parrots were brought to and traded in New Mexico in prehistoric times because their feathers were considered sacred.

Around 2010, Frances brought her distinctive egg gourd ornaments to Susan's Christmas Shop. Since then they have become one of the most popular locally made ornaments. Her husband helps by making curved wooden antlers for the "Mountain Sheep" egg gourd ornaments. These are some of the most creative and imaginative ornaments made by a local artist at Susan's Christmas Shop at the present time.

EPILOGUE

Creativity can be found at every level of society and culture. Some of the artists have degrees from art schools and others simply have a need to create. I love dealing with talented people. I value the long friendships that have resulted, both with the artists and with my customers. It has been my privilege to find creative, beautifully crafted Christmas items for so many years, and to offer them to the public out of such a small intimate space. My reward is seeing the pleasure they bring to my customers. I hope this book has added to that pleasure.

Because Christmas comes once a year, the handmade ornaments and nativities that charmed customers when they first saw them inside Susan's Christmas Shop continue to delight each time they are brought out at Christmas. They gradually become old friends we are pleased to see again. After many years of use at Christmastime, they may even become treasured heirlooms to be handed down to the next generation.